THE
FOOD
DOCTOR
EVERYDAY
DIET
COOKBOOK

THE FOOD DOCTOR EVERYDAY DIET COOKBOOK

Ian Marber Dip ION

Recipes by Rowena Paxton Dip ION

Keep in touch and stay in shape

Sign up at **www.dk.com/fooddoctortips** to receive
a monthly email full of encouragement from
Ian Marber, The Food Doctor

For more information on The Food Doctor, visit
www.thefooddoctor.com

LONDON, NEW YORK, MELBOURNE, MUNICH AND DELHI

For my wonderful sisters, Julia and Jacqueline, and their loved ones

Project Editor Susannah Steel
Project Designer Jo Grey
Senior Art Editor Anne Fisher
Managing Art Editor Marianne Markham
Managing Editor Penny Warren
Operations Publishing Manager Gillian Roberts
DTP Designer Sonia Charbonnier
Production Controller Luca Frassinetti
Art Director Carole Ash
Publishing Director Mary-Clare Jerram
Food stylist and home economist Pippin Britz
Photographer Sian Irvine

First published in Great Britain in 2006 by
Dorling Kindersley Limited,
80 Strand, London WC2R 0RL

A Penguin Company

2 4 6 8 10 9 7 5 3 1

Copyright © 2006 Dorling Kindersley Limited, London
Text copyright © 2006 Ian Marber

Always consult your health practitioner before starting a nutrition programme if you have any health concerns.

All rights reserved. No part of this publication may be reproduced, stored in a retrieval system, or transmitted in any form by any means, electronic, mechanical, photocopying, recording or otherwise, without the prior written permission of the copyright owner.

A CIP catalogue record for this book is available from the British Library

ISBN 10: 1-4053-1405-2
ISBN 13: 978-1-4053-1405-3

Colour reproduced by
Colourscan, Singapore
Printed and bound in Singapore by
Star Standard

Discover more at
www.dk.com

Contents

Recipes

Having a **better understanding** of foods and **knowing** which **beneficial** foods to eat can **improve** your general **well-being**

Introduction

We have all become increasingly aware that what we put in our mouths has a direct and profound impact on our health. So how should we eat to stay healthy for the longer term?

Every day it seems that newspapers are full of stories about the benefits of eating well, but we have to be sure we understand what "eating well" means. Many people will judge the state of their own health by whether or not they are overweight, since these days we seem to believe that being slim – or at least being slimmer – is the outward manifestation of being healthy. Yet this isn't always the case. If losing weight is your only goal, there are countless diets that can claim to help you (you've probably tried most of them) and their focus is purely on weight loss. Other benefits take second place. In other words, you can lose weight with unhealthy diets that rely on low-calorie processed foods or on high-fat and high-protein diets, none of which promote the best of health.

So to eat well means more than just losing weight. I believe that The Food Doctor Everyday Diet stands head and shoulders above most other eating plans because it provides benefits for your cardiovascular, digestive and immune system, as well as promoting consistent, appropriate weight loss. It will also improve the way you look and feel and increase your energy levels, to name just three of the welcome benefits. Other side-effects of following my 10 principles *(see pp.10–15)* include:

- No more ricocheting from one diet to another
- No guilt
- No shame
- No failure
- No fad diets.

The benefits of eating well

I am frequently asked what sort of symptoms drive private clients to book consultations at The Food Doctor clinic. These include fatigue, bloating, poor sleep quality, headaches, low concentration, deteriorating memory, cold hands and feet, thinning hair, cracked nails, constipation, wind… the list goes on. We know from the feedback from thousands of clients we have met that many of the conditions they describe have been alleviated and managed through improved nutrition. By following my simple plan of minimizing refined sugars, processed foods and saturated fats, and eating wholesome food rich in fibre, essential fats, vitamins and minerals, my clients have reported the disappearance of such day-to-day symptoms. It's also common for these clients to experience improvements in their health in areas that they had not anticipated. Typically, they benefit from clearer skin, improved quality of sleep, sharper memory recall, lower cholesterol, consistent energy levels, fewer colds, better digestion, sparkly eyes and, of course, weight loss. The simple truth is that eating an optimum diet can reap a wide range of rewards.

"I've been dieting since I was 13. I just wanted to stop the dieting and eat differently and sensibly long-term, have good health, lose some weight and be able to maintain it. Now I can achieve all these goals."

Alison

Cooking with confidence

In putting together this cook book, I wanted to show you how The Food Doctor principles can be easily adapted to preparing and storing food. The recipes underline just how easy it is to make these principles work for you. Take the 10 principles to heart and before long they'll become second nature. These recipes show you how to enjoy making delicious, simple food. You don't have to worry about weighing food, counting scores or learning the values of certain foods, all of which take the joy out of eating. Remember, there is no magic in any one food so if a recipe contains something you don't like, substitute it for another ingredient from the same food group. I have offered alternatives throughout the book to help you, but it's your food you are preparing so be creative and make things easy for yourself.

Making the recipes work for you

The recipes have been divided up into various sections to give you some gentle guidance. So, for example, if you find that you are tired and hungry when you get home at the end of the day and think that you don't have anything to eat, take a look at the recipes designed for such situations on pages 74–83. You can either follow recipes to the letter or

This book is designed to give **you** the **freedom** and **inspiration** to cook **healthy meals** with **confidence**

If you follow **the 10 principles** of **The Food Doctor Everyday Diet,** you'll **lose weight** at a sustainable rate and **feel great**

use them as a template, a suggestion to guide you towards great eating for life. Some golden rules to remember are:

- If you are making a dish, cook extra quantities to freeze for another day or to eat as snacks.
- Be creative with herbs and spices to add variety and flavour.
- Don't use any salt, as the dishes don't require them.
- Adapt any recipes to suit your lifestyle, tastes and budget.

The recipes in *The Food Doctor Diet* and *The Food Doctor Everyday Diet* have proven really popular, and I have had some welcome feedback telling me that whole families are enjoying them. All the recipes in this book are suitable for families, so you won't have the hassle of preparing different food for yourself. Just remember that children don't need to limit their intake of starchy carbohydrates at evening mealtimes.

Getting the right balance

You may be aware that I excluded puddings from my previous books, but I am really pleased to have included some delicious desserts here to eat after a main meal. One word of caution, however: they are best enjoyed only occasionally, for two reasons. Firstly, they add to the total carbohydrate load of a meal, which you must bear in mind when planning a meal. Secondly, I believe that eating sweet food perpetuates a desire for sugar, and avoiding sugar is one of my principles. My recipes are sweetened with fruit juice so they aren't bad for you, but by eating in the way that I map out you should minimize your desire for sweet foods. So please don't undo your good work by having desserts too often.

"It's really easy to follow the 80:20 rule. You can eat chocolate and a bag of chips, but I don't really fancy eating them anymore because I've been eating healthily."

Aly

Whilst *The Food Doctor Everyday Cook Book* recipes will encourage healthy, appropriate weight loss, please bear in mind that what we are aiming for is a sensible goal. Images of thin celebrities do little for one's self-esteem, so rather than try to emulate them and battle with feelings of failure, adopt a realistic, positive attitude and view this book as an easy, effective way to help you eat well and feel better for your life ahead.

10 Principles:Q&A

The 10 Food Doctor principles are my essential guidelines for how to eat sensibly and lose weight. Don't pick and choose these principles: they must all be part of your lifestyle plan if you want to feel and look better and have a healthier attitude to food. The questions listed here are among those frequently asked by my clients, and the answers might help to clarify any queries you may have.

PRINCIPLE 1

Eat protein with complex carbs

Combine three food groups in the right proportions: 40 per cent protein, 40 per cent complex vegetable carbohydrates and 20 per cent complex starchy carbohydrates.

Q How do I make sure I get the food proportions right?

A It's not an exact method, but the size of your protein should fit roughly in the palm of your hand. Vegetables will make up a portion of more or less the same size, with starchy carbs such as brown rice completing the meal. It's so easy that you'll soon be able to judge the ratios quickly. Just remember to omit starchy carbs and have a larger portion of vegetables if you eat dinner after 7.30pm.

Q I'm not a fan of vegetables. Can I just leave them out?

A You really do need the fibre and nutrients that vegetables contain, but if you are used to eating plain boiled food, experiment with new ways of preparing vegetables. There are several interesting recipes for vegetables throughout this book, so be brave. If it's the texture of vegetables you don't like, try making a simple purée to start with by briefly whizzing cooked peas or spinach in a blender.

Q I feel hungry in the evenings. Can I still eat my usual helping of potato or pasta to stop me picking at food later?

A Rather than eat excess complex carbohydrates in the evening, leave a small portion of your main meal and eat it later, or include a very small serving of pasta or rice with your evening meal.

Q Can you eat too much protein?

A It is possible to eat too much protein, which is why I have limited my recommendation to no more than 40 per cent. Excess protein creates an acidic environment, which the body will compensate for by taking minerals, especially calcium, from the bones to make it more alkaline. This can actually weaken bones in the longer term.

Q What exactly is the glycaemic index? Should I know more about it?

A The glycaemic index (GI) identifies the rate at which individual foods are broken down into glucose by the body. As excess glucose triggers insulin, those foods with a high GI rating lead to excess insulin. Avoiding this is a major part of my plan. Simple carbohydrates are the quickest foods to be broken down so they have a high GI. Complex carbohydrates take longer, while protein and essential fats are broken down slowly and so have a low GI rating. For more details on the GI index, take a look at www.thefooddoctor.com.

PRINCIPLE 2

Stay hydrated

Aim to drink at least a litre and a half of water a day in addition to other fluids.

Q Do hot drinks count towards my fluid intake?

A Hot drinks do count, but coffee can have a very mild diuretic effect so don't have too much (remember the 80:20 principle). Herbal teas, decaffeinated tea and coffee and soups are all appropriate choices for warm fluids.

Q Can I still drink alcohol?

A Alcohol is perhaps the ultimate simple carbohydrate, and is broken down and absorbed very rapidly. Furthermore, as it is a liquid it doesn't require much digestion and so affects blood glucose levels very quickly. I suggest having a glass or two of wine a day, but only with food, as this will slow down the absorption. However, spirits are not ideal, especially if mixed with juice or carbonated drinks.

Q Do soft drinks count?

A Soft drinks are nearly always sugared. Diet versions may be sugar-free, but they contain artificial sweeteners that perpetuate cravings for sweet food, so I don't recommend them at all.

PRINCIPLE 3

Eat a wide variety of food

Introduce two new healthy foods to your shopping trolley every week to encourage a positive relationship with beneficial foods.

Q I'm not very adventurous with my food. Can I take a vitamin pill instead?

A Absolutely not. A supplement should do exactly what it says it does, that is, supplement the diet, not replace it. Real food supplies nutritious benefits that pills just can't. If you aren't especially adventurous, try to buy one new food a month. You'll find that the effort will be very worthwhile.

Q I hate food shopping and I tend to just grab what I know I'll like to eat. Can I still buy my usual favourites as well as two new foods a week?

A Of course, don't take on any challenge that you can't achieve, as it can lead to a sense of frustration and failure. Fit your food shopping around your weekly schedule, and ensure that you have plenty of storecupboard foods at home in case you run out of fresh food. I've included some easy storecupboard recipes for you in Chapter four (see pp.74–83).

Q I am allergic to some of the ingredients in your recipes, so can I substitute them with other foods?

A Yes. If you react badly to any food, don't eat it. Just replace it with another food from the same food group. If you are concerned about food allergies or intolerances, seek the advice of a nutrition therapist and look at my website for more information on what can cause reactions to food.

PRINCIPLE 4

Fuel up frequently

Eat the right foods little and often to give you a constant supply of energy throughout the day while you continue to lose weight.

Q Do I have to eat a snack at the same time every day even if I'm not hungry?

A Ideally, you should eat a light meal every three hours or so, but if you can't do this every day then do eat something between main meals. This ensures that you won't reach a low in your blood glucose levels, which can lead to hunger and poor food choices. So even if you aren't hungry, please have something to eat, however small it might be, in order that your metabolic rate is maintained.

Q I'm often out on business. How do I eat snacks if I'm on the go all day?

A This is a common problem, especially as most business meetings usually provide coffee and sweet biscuits. A piece of fruit will suffice – preferably a hard fruit such as an apple or pear. Excuse yourself for a moment to eat it, or have it in the meeting; no-one will mind. The trick is to make sure that you always have something with you in your bag or briefcase. The Food Doctor snack bars are designed for this purpose *(see p.16)*.

Q I eat lots of fruit between meals, but I still feel hungry. Why is this?

A Some fruits have a high GI so they are broken down into glucose rapidly, leading to insulin production and subsequent low blood glucose levels, which you experience as hunger. Add protein to your snack and avoid fruits with a high GI.

PRINCIPLE 5

Eat breakfast

A balanced breakfast supplies you with fuel to maintain energy levels and sets your metabolism up for the day, which helps to control your weight.

Q I can't face breakfast in the morning. Does it matter?

A Ask yourself if skipping breakfast has helped you in the past and if, as I suspect, the answer is "no", resolve to start every day with something to eat. Even the smallest meal, such as a small pot of natural yoghurt with some seeds and a few bites of an apple, can help you achieve your goals. It will make a major difference to your eating patterns for the rest of the day. Always ensure that you have a little protein with your complex carbohydrates when you do eat. If you get up early and eat breakfast when you get to work, the same advice applies.

Q I often skip breakfast at weekends and have brunch instead. Is this OK?

A Don't be a slave to your diet, so go ahead and enjoy your weekend brunch. However, I would still suggest that you eat something small early in the day, rather than waiting for brunch. Remember it's not the total amount of food you eat in a day that will support you, it's what you eat, and how much, at regular intervals that will make a difference to your success with The Food Doctor Everyday Diet.

Q Can I still have my usual morning cup of coffee?

A Yes, do have your coffee if you want, but only with your breakfast. If you have caffeine at the start of the day without food, it acts like a high GI food, raising glucose levels that lead to that familiar dip in energy soon after. Decaffeinated coffee is a compromise, but it's not ideal, so I suggest that you still drink it with a meal or snack.

Q Can I still have toast and marmalade for breakfast if I use a low-sugar variety of marmalade?

A I am glad to see that you are avoiding products containing sugar, but that's only part of the picture. Whilst the toast may have fibre in it, the marmalade is still a simple carbohydrate. If you ask yourself, "Where's the protein?" at every meal and snack, you will be able to improve your usual breakfast choices. Have some nut butter or The Food Doctor Omega Seed Butter with your toast instead to make it an ideal breakfast meal.

PRINCIPLE 6

Avoid sugar
Sugar breaks down into glucose extremely quickly in the body, contributing to fat production and weight gain.

Q Can I still eat dried fruits and honey?

A Honey and dried fruits have a fairly high GI rating, so they aren't ideal. Many clients tell me that they have enjoyed significantly reduced sugar cravings when they avoid honey and dried fruits.

Q My kids always want dessert when we eat family meals. Can I join them?

A Following the 10 principles will minimize your cravings for sweet food, but I have included some recipes for low GI desserts in this book so that if you make them for your kids, having a little won't be a disaster. Do bear in mind that having sweet food leads to wanting more, and on it goes.

Q I've been eating lots of low-fat products in an effort to lose weight. Is it alright to keep eating these foods?

A Low-fat foods are generally processed and are likely to contain a fair degree of sugar. Ask yourself if they have previously helped you to lose weight and keep that weight off. As they probably haven't, I suggest that you avoid such products.

PRINCIPLE 7

Exercise is essential
Exercise increases your metabolic rate – the speed at which your body uses up food as energy – aiding a weight-loss programme. Frequent exercise also improves your health and your response to stress.

Q I just don't get time to exercise during the week. Is going for a walk at the weekend enough?

A It's hard to fit a workout into your busy week, I know, but even a brisk walk every other day – or anything that raises the heart rate consistently for a minimum of 20 minutes – will do. Exercising three times a week in addition to your weekend walks is the ideal answer if you want sustained weight-loss.

Q I exercise a lot, sometimes every day, but I don't seem to get results.

A It's quite possible that you are over-exercising, which can cause the metabolic rate to respond in the same way that it does with under-eating. Reduce your exercise levels slowly, aim for a maximum of four sessions a week and include stretching, and perhaps some gentle yoga, in your routine.

Q What is metabolic rate?

A This is the amount of energy expended in a given time. Food is converted into glucose, which is used as fuel to create energy, so your input of food and output of energy must be balanced to achieve weight loss. However, eating too little can alert the metabolic rate to potential "famine", which is easily avoided by following the 10 principles.

Q If I exercise, I want to eat more. Is this normal, and what should I do?

A Not only this it normal, it's a good sign that your metabolic rate is asking you to eat more to create a healthy balance in your diet. I suggest that you increase your portion sizes very slightly to meet the demands of your increased energy output.

PRINCIPLE 8

Follow the 80:20 rule

Follow the 10 principles 80 per cent of the time and enjoy treats or social occasions 20 per cent of the time without feeling guilty or worrying about straying from the diet.

Q I have a sweet tooth, so if I eat healthily all day, can I eat a small bar of chocolate every night?

A If you keep your glucose levels in check, which will happen naturally when you follow my plan, your sugar cravings will become negligible. If you do want to eat something sweet to eat from time to time, have a couple of squares of high-quality dark chocolate (one with at least 70 per cent cocoa content), but do remember that eating chocolate will lead to a desire for more sugary foods.

Q I get depressed if I eat something I know is not good for me, but I can't stop myself. Then I eat more forbidden foods. How do I stop the cycle?

A This feeling is one that is usually associated with old-fashioned diets. Clients who follow The Food Doctor Everyday Diet say that they don't want to eat foods that make them feel as if they have failed. If you keep eating foods that you know won't benefit you, think about why you eat them and work with an appropriate specialist to end this cycle of sin and reward. Some clients report that hypnotherapy has worked for them; others find that cleaning their teeth helps. Find a solution that will work for you.

Q Does the 80:20 rule refer to quantity or frequency?

A It applies to what you eat and how often. You can have desserts two or three times a week at the most, but certainly not during the first three weeks of following my plan. And choosing to have a "20-per cent treat" at every meal will simply keep you trapped in an unhealthy cycle.

PRINCIPLE 9

Make time to eat

Taking time to eat your food and chew each mouthful properly can benefit your digestive health. It can also make your food become more satisfying and filling.

Q I have a demanding job and my stress levels are high all day, so I try to grab a quick lunch. Can I eat a bigger meal in the evening to compensate?

A Stress is one of the factors that naturally raises glucose levels due to the action of adrenaline. By following my diet plan and making time to eat proper meals and snacks at regular intervals, you can help combat high levels of stress. In other words, The Food Doctor Everyday Diet will make things feel easier for you, not the other way round. Over-eating at any meal will not compensate for missed snacks and meals, so having a large dinner is not the solution. In fact, it's more likely that such actions will lead to a low in your blood glucose levels which you'll experience as hunger.

Q I have a lengthy journey home each day so there is a long gap between my afternoon snack and dinner. Is this acceptable or am I getting it wrong?

A This plan has to fit in with your lifestyle, but you can keep your glucose levels steady by eating a healthy snack on the journey home. A piece of fruit with a few nuts will do, or buy a generously filled sandwich and discard half the bread to make a snack with a favourable ratio of carbohydrates to protein. If you can't manage to do either as you travel home, make sure that you have something to eat immediately before you leave work in order to fill that long gap until dinner.

Q I am too tired to cook when I get in from work and my weekends are always busy, so how do I follow your plan of eating proper meals?

A You don't have to cook, simply prepare. An egg on toast will do, or some fish with vegetables. Stock your storecupboard and fridge with basics such as eggs, canned fish and chick-peas, vegetables, flat breads and crackers, or make use of the Essential shopping lists on pages 154–155 and be inspired by the Food fast recipes in Chapter two *(see pp.28–61).*

PRINCIPLE 10

Eat fat to lose fat

The body needs essential fats to function properly. Eat less saturated fat and include more essential fats in your diet instead.

Q Can I take a supplement of essential fats (omega 3 and 6)?

A You can take a supplement, but I would prefer that essential fats come from your food. Supplements shouldn't replace missing elements in your diet. I suggest consulting a nutritional therapist for advice on supplements – the cost will be recouped by not wasting money on unnecessary supplements.

Q I know fish is good for me, but I don't like it. What else can I eat?

A This problem applies to vegans and vegetarians too. Essential fats are found in nuts, seeds, oils and avocado, to name just a few foods. Omega 3 is also found in purslane, a herb that is suitable for vegans and which can be grown easily in a window box or a garden. In some cases a supplement might be appropriate, but do consult a professional first.

Q I often crave butter or some crisps. Why is this, and am I allowed them?

A Fat has a consistency that gives us a satisfying eating sensation, known in the food industry as "mouth feel". Do have a little unsalted butter on your bread or a few crisps if you must, but I have found that when clients increase their intake of essential fats (which you will do naturally when you follow my plan), their food provides that satisfying mouth feel sensation and minimizes any cravings for other non-essential, or saturated, fats.

The Food Doctor Everyday Diet notes

On The Food Doctor Everyday Diet plan you eat nutritious foods little and often, which improves digestive health and encourages sustainable weight loss. It's a food plan that suits all situations and lifestyles. Many people have now tried the diet, and welcomed its success.

Dear Ian,

For the first time ever I feel fitter, in control and very positive. When you have tried one diet after another you begin to feel very despondent and, to be honest, don't know which way to turn next. I'm so glad I took the plunge and followed your diet advice, it's one of the best decisions I ever made.

Cathy

Dear Ian

I've lost 1 stone (7.3 kilos) by following your diet. It's not a difficult diet to follow, it's more of a change to lifestyle – improving the way you eat – than a diet. It fits in with pretty much everything, and you don't feel guilty because there's nothing that's off-limits.

Stuart

Healthy choices from The Food Doctor

The Food Doctor Everyday Diet promotes eating little and often as the key to keeping your energy levels consistent and achieving successful weight loss. These Food Doctor products can help to keep your diet healthy and your metabolism in balance.

Breakfast products:
- Cereal mix, Muesli mix and Porridge mix

Seed mixes:
- Original, Chilli and Garlic, Fennel and Caraway, Rosemary and Onion, Thyme and Sage

Snacks:
- Dry Roasted Soya Nuts
- High Bran and Seed Bagels
- Mixed Cereal Puffed Crackers

Snack bars:
- Apple and Walnut, Apricot and Almond, Pineapple and Banana, Fig and Mango, Tomato and Chilli

Food Doctor basics:
- Essential Omega Seed Butter
- Essential Omega Seed Oil
- Omega-3 Yoghurt
- Aloe Vera Yoghurt with pre-biotic

The Food Doctor plan was written after **working** for many thousands of hours **with people** who want to **lose weight**

Hi Ian,

I wanted to write and let you know that I've lost a little over 4½lbs (2 kilos) on your diet. I started with The Food Doctor Seven-day Diet, which was quite hard (I'm not a big soup fan) and it felt like a long seven days, but the results were worthwhile. I've now only got to lose 9lbs (4 kilos) to get to my ideal weight for my height.

Cheryl

Hi Ian,

You should know that, at 61, I am a seasoned dieter from way back. In general I eat healthily, but far too much, and tend to comfort myself with confectionery on solo business car journeys.

Imagine my surprise as the pointer on the scale dropped steadily on each day of your Seven-day Diet; I did enlarge the portions just a bit, and added more green vegetables and salad, but no major cheats, and I was delighted to find that I had no need to curtail my sessions at the gym.

By Saturday I had dropped 7lbs (1.4 kilos), and I could see and feel it. So I had to email you to congratulate you.

I am based in an office, but I am out and about intermittently. Yet there was one day last week when I found myself furtively eating my mid-morning snack in my parked car. I am sure I can continue to eat these snacks during my working day if they are going to continue to have this beneficial effect.

Judy

Dear Ian

I've lost 3 stone (19 kilos) following the principles. It's been really easy. It's not a difficult plan to follow. You're not told what to eat and when to eat it. It's second nature now.

Aly

If you follow **The Food Doctor Everyday Diet** principles, you should **succeed** in your goal to **lose weight** and feel **healthy**

Eat breakfast

It's essential that you have a balanced breakfast. These easy recipes are excellent examples of the best way to start the day.

Breakfast crunch with fresh fruit Ⓥ

Use a heavy, wide-based saucepan or frying pan to toast these seeds and grains. It's best to toast the ingredients separately, as they will brown at different rates. Choose fruits that are in season. Serves two.

ready in 20 minutes

2 palmfuls fresh fruit

2 tablespoons live natural low-fat yoghurt

2 tablespoons mixed pumpkin and sesame seeds

For the toasted grains and seeds:

50g (2oz) quinoa seeds

50g (2oz) quinoa flakes

100g (3½oz) barley flakes

50g (2oz) raisins

100g (3½oz) oat flakes

50g (2oz) hemp seeds, shelled

Toast the quinoa, barley and oats first. Place the saucepan over a medium-high heat until hot. Cook each ingredient for a few minutes until evenly toasted to a light brown, tossing and turning them frequently so they do not burn. The quinoa seeds will pop so you may need to cover the pan.

Mix the toasted ingredients in a wide, shallow bowl and leave to cool, turning occasionally. Once cool, stir in the raisins and hemp seeds. Store in a large airtight jar in a cool, dark place.

When you are ready to eat breakfast, put 3 tablespoons of the toasted mix in each bowl, add a tablespoon of natural yoghurt and scatter fresh fruit and seeds over the top of each serving.

Spiced porridge Ⓥ

This unusual variation on porridge makes an ideal start to your day. Choose whichever mix of flakes you like, and adapt the spices accordingly to suit your individual tastes. This recipe serves two.

| ready in **10** minutes |

1 star anise

200ml (7fl oz) boiling water

50g (2oz) mixed flakes: oats, millet, quinoa, barley, rice, etc. (use a mix of large and small flakes for an interesting texture)

¼ teaspoon ground cinnamon

¼ teaspoon ground ginger

Juice ½ lemon

2 tablespoons live natural low-fat yoghurt

Zest ½ orange

1 apple, cored and grated

2 tablespoons sunflower seeds (optional)

Apples are an ideal choice of fruit, as they provide the body with sustained levels of energy when eaten with some protein.

Put the star anise in a jug and pour the boiling water over it. Leave to stand for 5 minutes.

Put the mixed flakes in a saucepan. Add the ground spices and lemon juice. Remove the star anise from the jug, pour the water into the saucepan and stir well. Simmer very gently for about 3 minutes until the flakes are soft and the mix has a thick, soft consistency.

Stir in the yoghurt and serve topped with the apple, orange zest and sunflower seeds.

Blueberry cheese Ⓥ

Fromage frais is a good choice for breakfast because it has a higher proportion of protein to carbohydrate than yoghurt. Mix with blueberries and seeds for an instant, delicious meal. Serves two.

ready in **1** minute

6 tablespoons reduced fat fromage frais

6 tablespoons mixed seeds (pumpkin, sesame, sunflower, hemp, ground linseeds – choose at least two)

4 tablespoons blueberries

Divide the fromage frais between two bowls. Top each serving with 3 tablespoons of seeds and 2 tablespoons of blueberries and serve.

Note: there are various mixes of seeds available, including The Food Doctor range *(see pp.16, 160)*.

Ham and cheese corn fritters

When you need something substantial on a cold morning, this tasty, protein-rich dish is excellent. You can experiment with other toppings, such as scrambled egg, or smoked salmon. Serves two.

ready in **10** minutes

2 corn fritters *(see p.25)*
2 tablespoons reduced-fat fromage frais
2 extra thin slices good-quality smoked ham, cut in strips
2 medium tomatoes, chopped
A few toasted sesame seeds

Spread the warm fritter with the fromage frais. Top with the ham, tomato and the toasted seeds and serve.

Easy egg breakfasts

Eggs are packed with vitamins, folate and calcium, are high in protein and have minimal saturated fat, so they are an ideal start to your day. In fact, these recipes are so versatile and tasty that you can have them as a light lunch or for supper as well. All recipes serve two.

Keep some **fresh eggs** in the **fridge,** as they are an **excellent** source of **protein**

Poached egg on asparagus and mushrooms

Poached egg on asparagus & mushrooms Ⓥ

ready in **15** minutes

50g (2oz) medium-sized brown mushrooms

100g (3½oz) asparagus tips

A drizzle of olive oil

1 tablespoon cider vinegar

2 eggs

Freshly ground black pepper

Preheat the oven to 180°C/350°F/gas mark 4.

Slice the mushrooms diagonally to make large flat slices. Place them on a baking tray and drizzle a tiny amount of olive oil over each slice so that they are lightly coated. Bake in the oven for 10 minutes.

Put the asparagus into a small saucepan, pour boiling water on top and simmer for about a minute or so until the tips are al dente. Drain.

Heat a large pan of water and add the vinegar. Once the water is simmering, crack the eggs into the water or into poaching rings and cook until the egg whites are set. Remove with a slotted spoon.

Arrange the mushrooms on a plate, layer the asparagus over them and top with the poached egg. Season with black pepper and serve with wholemeal toast or corn fritters (see right) if needed.

Eggy bread with seeds Ⓥ

ready in **10** minutes

2 eggs

2 tablespoons The Food Doctor Original Seed Mix, coarsely ground, or grind 2 tablespoons mixed pumpkin, sunflower, linseeds and sesame seeds

Freshly ground black pepper

A drizzle of olive oil

2 thick slices of wholemeal, rye or gluten-free bread

2 medium tomatoes

Lightly beat the eggs, seeds and black pepper together and pour the mixture onto a deep dinner plate. Soak the bread well in the egg mix.

Lightly oil a non-stick frying pan and, once the pan is hot, lift the egg-soaked bread and place in the pan to gently brown on both sides. If there is any egg mix left on the plate, pour it on top of the bread while the first side is browning.

If you have time, roast the tomatoes (see p.26), otherwise chop them coarsely, pile them on top of the eggy bread and serve.

Poached egg on a corn fritter Ⓥ

ready in **15** minutes

2 eggs

1 tablespoon cider vinegar

For the corn fritters (makes 4):

100g (3½oz) maize flour

1 fresh egg

1 tablespoon olive oil

75ml (3fl oz) milk or water

70g (2½oz) canned sweetcorn (without added sugar), drained and rinsed

½ teaspoon ground caraway seeds or ground fennel seeds

Freshly ground black pepper

To prepare the corn fritters, put the flour in a bowl and make a well in the middle. Break the egg into the well and pour in the olive oil. Beating continually, add the milk gradually to give a smooth, thick batter. Stir in the sweetcorn and spices and season with black pepper.

Brush a non-stick frying pan with a little olive oil and pour in a quarter of the mixture. The batter should be thick enough not to run when poured. Brown one side over a medium heat, flip over and brown the other. Once cooked, keep warm.

Poach the eggs (see left) and serve on the fritters.

Roast tomatoes with spinach & ham

The best way to retain the nutrients in vegetables such as spinach is to steam them. If you use a bamboo steamer over a pan of boiling water, it only takes a few minutes to cook the spinach. Serves two.

ready in 15 minutes

8 cherry tomatoes (approx 160g/5½oz)

A drizzle of olive oil

Freshly ground black pepper

75g (2½oz) baby spinach leaves

2 slices wholemeal or rye toast

Grated fresh nutmeg or a pinch ground nutmeg

2 extra thin slices ham, cut into fine strips

Preheat the oven to 180°C/350°F/gas mark 4.

Put the tomatoes on a small baking tray, add a drizzle of olive oil, toss the tomatoes in the oil and season with black pepper. Roast for 10–15 minutes, by which time the tomatoes should be collapsing.

Put the washed spinach in a steamer and cook for about 3 minutes, until the leaves are wilted. Remove and drain.

Drizzle each slice of toast with a little olive oil, layer the spinach on top and grate a little nutmeg over it. Add the ham, place the tomatoes on top and serve.

Mixed-grill pancakes

Pancakes are a deliciously different alternative to toast. If you want a vegetarian dish, use toasted seeds *(see p.127)* instead of liver. Any excess pancakes can be refrigerated for a couple of days. Serves two.

ready in 20 minutes

2 medium tomatoes, quartered

2 medium mushrooms, quartered

1 medium courgette, cut into thick slices

2 tablespoons olive oil

Freshly ground black pepper

100g (3½oz) liver (chicken, calf, lamb or venison)

For the pancakes:

100g (3½oz) buckwheat flour

1 large egg

300ml (½ pint) milk and water, mixed (or all water)

Freshly ground black pepper

½ teaspoon dried Herbes de Provence *(see p.150)*

For the sauce:

3 teaspoons soy sauce

3 teaspoons Dijon mustard

1 tablespoon lemon juice

To make the pancakes, put the flour into a large bowl, make a well in the middle and break in the egg. Add the fluid gradually, using a whisk, until the mix resembles thin cream. Beat in the black pepper and herbs.

Heat a non-stick pancake pan until it's hot, brush with olive oil and pour in about 75ml (3fl oz) of the pancake mix. Cook for a couple of minutes until the pancake sets, then it flip over and brown the other side. Once cooked, turn onto a plate, cover and keep warm while you cook the rest of the pancakes.

Put the tomatoes, mushrooms and courgette slices in a grill pan, toss them in a tablespoon of olive oil and season with black pepper. Grill the vegetables under a medium grill for about 10 minutes, turning frequently, until the courgette slices turn golden and the tomatoes and mushrooms are soft.

Heat another tablespoon of olive oil in a frying pan and gently cook the liver – this will take 4–6 minutes, depending on the thickness of the meat. It should be nicely browned on the outside, but still slightly pink in the middle. Cut the meat into several small slices.

Mix the sauce ingredients together and pour into a jug.

Put a wrap back into the pancake pan, heat it gently, turn it over and put half the grilled vegetables on one side. Top with half the liver and pour over a little of the sauce. Fold the pancake in two and it leave in the pan for a couple of minutes to warm through. Turn out onto a plate, heat and fill the second pancake and serve.

Cultivated mushrooms are among the freshest of vegetables available. Brown mushrooms tend to have a firmer texture and nuttier flavour.

Food fast

When time is short, these recipes demonstrate just how simple it is to apply my principles and cook delicious, healthy meals quickly.

Simple smoothies

For breakfasts and snacks on the go, nothing beats an energy-boosting smoothie. This eclectic range of smoothie recipes caters to all tastes. From the sweet Tropical carrot smoothie to the tangy High-energy smoothie, all these drinks are vitamin-packed and filling. Serves two.

Carrot & caraway smoothie Ⓥ

`ready in` **3** `minutes`

2 tablespoons The Food Doctor Fennel and Caraway Seed mix, or use ½ teaspoon each fennel and caraway seeds and 2 tablespoons mixed pumpkin and sunflower seeds

150ml (¼ pint) natural low-fat yoghurt

150ml (¼ pint) carrot juice

½ avocado

Juice 1 lemon

Juice 1 orange

Grind the seed mix in a seed or coffee grinder.

Put all the ingredients into a blender and whizz together for a few seconds before serving.

Carrot & caraway smoothie

Vegetable smoothie

Vegetable smoothie Ⓥ

ready in 2 minutes

150g (5oz) cucumber

1 medium tomato

50g (2oz) red pepper

100ml (3½fl oz) carrot juice

75ml (3fl oz) apple juice

Juice 1 lemon

3 tablespoons live natural low-fat yoghurt

Whizz the vegetables with the carrot and fruit juices in a blender for a few seconds. Do not sieve as this will remove valuable fibre. Stir in the yoghurt and serve.

Tropical carrot smoothie Ⓥ

ready in 3 minutes

150ml (¼ pint) live natural low-fat yoghurt

150ml (¼ pint) carrot juice

1 good, peeled chunk each mango and papaya

Seeds and flesh 1 passion fruit, scooped out of the skin (avoid the pith)

1 small cube fresh ginger, grated

25g (¾oz) raw unsalted cashew nuts

Combine all the ingredients in a blender and whizz together until smooth. Add more carrot juice if the mixture is too thick, and serve.

High-energy smoothie Ⓥ

ready in 10 minutes

½ avocado, stoned and peeled

150ml (¼ pint) live natural low-fat yoghurt

100ml (3½fl oz) good-quality apple juice

100ml (3½fl oz) water

A small handful watercress leaves

2–3 springs fresh mint

Juice ½ lemon

A few drops Tabasco

Put all the ingredients, except the Tabasco, in a blender and whizz together until smooth. Add a dash of Tabasco to taste and serve.

Tropical carrot smoothie

High-energy smoothie

The Food Doctor bagel toppings

These savoury toppings taste delicious on The Food Doctor High Bran and Seed Bagels, or on oatcakes or rye bread. Keep them in plastic containers in the fridge. You can also use these toppings as a side dish with grilled meat or fish. Each recipe makes enough for two bagels.

Feta cheese & roast pepper mash Ⓥ

| ready in | **5** | minutes |

50g (2oz) roast pepper slices (from a jar)

50g (2oz) feta cheese

Freshly ground black pepper

A few sprigs fresh parsley, chopped

Chop the peppers finely. Combine all the ingredients in a bowl and mash them roughly with a fork. Keeps in the fridge for two days.

Chick-pea & caramelized onion mash

Simple roasted tomatoes

Smoked fish mash

Smoked fish mash

ready in **5** minutes

50g (2oz) hot smoked fish
(supermarkets often sell cheap off-cuts
of mackerel, trout and salmon, etc.)

2 tablespoons reduced-fat fromage frais

A good handful watercress, chopped

1 tablespoon fresh dill, chopped

Juice ½ lemon

Freshly ground black pepper

Mash all the ingredients together
using a fork and season with a
generous grinding of black pepper.
You can also use this mash like a
dip and scoop it out of a bowl with
oatcakes or rye crackers. Will keep
fresh for 24 hours in the fridge.

Feta cheese
& roast pepper mash

Simple roasted tomatoes ⓥ

ready in **15** minutes

3 medium tomatoes, quartered

1 garlic clove, peeled

A drizzle of olive oil

Freshly ground black pepper

Lemon juice to taste

Preheat the oven to
180°C/350°F/gas mark 4.

Put the tomatoes and garlic in a
small baking tray, drizzle with the
oil, add a good grinding of black
pepper and toss to mix.

Roast for 10–15 minutes until the
tomatoes are collapsing. Toast the
bagels and then pile the tomatoes
on top, mashing them down a little.
Squeeze a little lemon juice over the
top of the tomatoes.

The tomatoes need a good strong-
tasting protein on top, so try one of
the following ingredients:

• marinated anchovies
• feta cheese
• lean smoked ham and mustard

Chick-pea & caramelized onion mash ⓥ

ready in **20** minutes

1x400g (13oz) can organic chick-peas

1 garlic clove

2 sprigs fresh sage

A pinch bouillon powder (or
¼ stock cube)

1 medium onion, finely sliced

3 tablespoons olive oil

1 teaspoon ground caraway seeds

1 tablespoon live natural low-fat yoghurt

2 tablespoons lemon juice

2 tablespoons fresh dill, chopped

Crumbled feta cheese as a garnish

Drain and rinse the chick-peas. Put
them in a saucepan with the garlic,
sage and bouillon powder, pour in
just enough water to cover the
chick-peas and bring to the boil.
Simmer gently for 15 minutes.

Meanwhile, heat a tablespoon of
olive oil in a saucepan, add the
onion and cook gently until soft.
Raise the heat to brown the onions
a little. Stir in the ground caraway
over a low heat, adding a little
more oil if it all binds too thickly.

Drain the chick-peas and remove
the herbs and garlic. Mash the
chick-peas with a fork or potato
masher, adding the olive oil and
yoghurt to soften the consistency.
Stir in the onions, lemon juice and
fresh dill. Pile onto two bagels with
a little feta cheese crumbled on top.

Lunch boxes

These salads are designed to be made the previous night or the morning before you go to work so that you can just reach for a nutritious meal at lunchtime. All recipes serve two, so you should be able to save yourself time by making enough lunch for two consecutive days.

Lentil & sprouted seed salad Ⓥ

| ready in **15** minutes |

100g (3½oz) dried red lentils, or 4 tablespoons canned lentils, rinsed and drained

200ml (7fl oz) vegetable stock *(see p.86)*

1 avocado, peeled and sliced

Fresh lemon juice to taste

100g (3½oz) sprouted seeds, rinsed and drained

100g (3½oz) cucumber, cut into thick matchstick pieces

½ red pepper, sliced

French dressing to taste

2–3 tablespoons fresh herbs, chopped

If you have time, put the dried lentils in a saucepan, add the stock and simmer for 5–10 minutes until soft but not collapsed. Rinse and drain. Otherwise, spoon the canned lentils into a bowl.

If you make this salad the night before, leave slicing the avocado and sprinkling it with lemon juice until the morning.

Add the sprouts, cucumber and red pepper to the lentils. Add French dressing to taste and toss well. Fold in the avocado and fresh herbs of your choice and pack the contents into a lunch box. For a change, add some hot smoked fish too.

Tomato, bulgar wheat & spinach salad Ⓥ

| ready in **15** minutes |

100g (3½oz) bulgar wheat, plus boiling vegetable stock to cover

2 tablespoons olive oil

1 garlic clove, finely chopped

100g (3½oz) baby spinach leaves, washed

Grated fresh nutmeg to taste

Juice 1 lemon

Freshly ground black pepper

12 baby tomatoes, halved

12 pitted black olives

100g (3½oz) feta cheese, cubed

Pour boiling stock over the bulgar wheat until it is just covered. Leave to stand for 10 minutes, then strain and squeeze it through a fine sieve.

Heat the oil in a frying pan and add the garlic. Soften over a low heat for 2 minutes. Add the spinach and stir over a medium heat until the spinach is wilted. Grate a little nutmeg over the spinach.

Combine the bulgar wheat and spinach with its oil in a bowl. Toss well, add the lemon juice and season with black pepper. Gently fold in the tomatoes, olives and feta cheese.

Put into a lunch box and go. The flavours improve if left for a couple of hours or more before eating.

Mixed bean salad Ⓥ

| ready in **5** minutes |

1x400g (13oz) can mixed beans, rinsed and drained

½ cucumber, coarsely chopped with the skin left on

2 medium tomatoes, each cut into six pieces

French dressing to taste

Freshly ground black pepper

100g (3½oz) feta cheese, cubed

2–3 tablespoons fresh mixed herbs of your choice, chopped (parsley, mint, chives, coriander or basil, depending on what is available)

1 flat bread *(see p.88)*, 2 oatcakes or 1 piece rye bread per person

Mix the beans, raw vegetables, French dressing and black pepper together in a bowl. Fold in the feta cheese and chopped herbs.

Put the contents into a lunch box and eat with the rye bread, oatcakes or flat bread if you have some stored in the fridge or freezer.

Mixed seeds

High-energy salad Ⓥ

ready in **10** minutes

4 eggs

2 medium tomatoes, quartered

4 closed white mushrooms, sliced

1 yellow pepper, cut into strips

2 raw baby carrots, washed

75g (2½oz) raw, bite-sized broccoli florets

75g (2½oz) raw, bite-sized cauliflower florets

4 tablespoons The Food Doctor Rosemary & Garlic Seed Mix, or use 4 tablespoons mixed pumpkin, sesame, sunflower and linseeds with ½ teaspoon garlic, chopped

1 flat bread *(see p.88)* or 1 corn fritter *(see p.21)* per person

Boil the eggs for 10 minutes until they are hard-boiled. cool them in cold water, then shell them and cut them in half.

Mix the other ingredients together, pack into a lunch box and place the eggs on top. Eat with the flat bread or corn fritter. Using the spiced Food Doctor seeds means that there is no need for dressing.

You can add any raw vegetables of your choice to change the mix, but keep the quantities high to give you enough energy.

Take a healthy **lunch box** to work so that you always make a **good food choice** at lunchtime

High-energy salad

Healthy soups

These soups, which range from a light, tasty broth to a hearty, filling soup, are low in fat and full of vitamins. Since they are all quick and easy to prepare, they are the perfect meal if you are pressed for time, or want something simple to eat. All recipes serve two.

Japanese broth

SERVING IDEAS

For lunch A slice of wholemeal or rye bread makes a filling accompaniment for any of these soups.

For dinner Omit the bread and add a handful of sunflower seeds, linseeds or pumpkin seeds to your bowl of soup for added protein instead.

Japanese broth Ⓥ

ready in **15** minutes

1.2 litres (2 pints) hot vegetable stock *(see p.86)*

100g (3½oz) carrots, cut into large matchstick pieces

100g (3½oz) baby sweetcorn, cut in half lengthways and across

100g (3½oz) mangetout

100g (3½oz) baby leeks (or spring onions), finely sliced

2cm (¾in) cube fresh ginger, finely grated

2 tablespoons rice wine

1 teaspoon soy sauce

1 teaspoon miso paste

Tabasco sauce to taste

A small handful fresh coriander, chopped

For the egg noodles:
2 eggs

2 tablespoons pumpkin seeds, coarsely ground

2 tablespoons water

Pour the hot stock into a saucepan, add the carrots and cook for 2 minutes. Add the corn, mangetout, leeks and grated ginger. Simmer for 10 minutes, then stir in the rice wine, soy sauce and miso paste.

To make the noodles, mix the eggs, seeds and water together and cook two thin, flat omelettes *(see p.138)*. Roll up each omelette and slice it across several times to make thin ribbons of egg.

Serve the hot soup in two bowls, topped with the egg ribbons and fresh coriander. Any leftover soup can be frozen for up to four weeks.

Pea & ginger soup Ⓥ

ready in **15** minutes

1 medium onion, finely chopped

¼ teaspoon cumin seeds

1 tablespoon olive oil

200g (7oz) frozen peas

1x400g (13oz) can butter beans, drained and rinsed

2cm (¾in) cube fresh ginger, finely grated

700ml (1¼ pints) chicken or vegetable stock *(see p.86)*

A small handful fresh coriander, chopped

A small handful fresh mint, chopped

Juice 1 lime

Freshly ground black pepper

2 tablespoons live natural low-fat yoghurt

3 spring onions, finely chopped

Heat the olive oil in a large saucepan, add the onion and cumin seeds and cook gently until the onion is soft but not coloured.

Add the peas, beans, ginger and stock, bring to the boil and lower the heat to a simmer. Add the fresh herbs and stir well. Simmer for about 5 minutes. Pour it all into a blender and zap until smooth.

Pour back into the saucepan and add the lime juice and black pepper.

Serve each portion with a swirl of yoghurt and the chopped spring onions sprinkled over the top.

You can also serve the soup chilled. Stir the yoghurt into the cold soup and garnish with the spring onions.

Salmon & sweet potato soup

ready in **20** minutes

2x150g (5oz) fillets salmon, skinned and cut into bite-sized pieces

Lemon juice to taste

Freshly ground black pepper

1 tablespoon olive oil

1 medium leek, trimmed and finely sliced

1 small bulb of Florence fennel, trimmed and finely sliced

200g (7oz) sweet potato, grated

75ml (3fl oz) dry white wine

600ml (1 pint) good fish stock (the better the stock, the better the soup)

2 tablespoons fresh dill, chopped (or 1 teaspoon dried dill)

2 tablespoons live natural low-fat yoghurt

Toss the salmon pieces in lemon juice and black pepper and set aside while you cook the vegetables.

Heat the oil in a wide-bottomed saucepan. Add the leek and fennel and soften for 5 minutes. Add the sweet potato, stir once and add the wine. Let it bubble for a couple of minutes, then stir in the stock and simmer for 15 minutes until the vegetables are cooked and the potatoes are collapsing into the liquid. Add the fish and chopped dill and simmer gently for 5 minutes until the fish is just cooked. Add seasoning to taste.

Ladle into two hot bowls and swirl the yoghurt into each serving.

Pestos for any meal

These are invaluable recipes, as they add flavour to any dish. Use a pesto as a sauce for grilled or baked fish, as a marinade or a dip, stir it into hot or cold quinoa for extra flavour or spread it over chicken breasts and cover with sliced tomatoes. All recipes serve two.

The Food Doctor special Ⓥ

ready in **2** minutes

2 tablespoons The Food Doctor Original Seed mix, or use 2 tablespoons mixed linseeds, pumpkin and sunflower seeds

3 tablespoons olive oil

A small handful watercress (about 20g/1oz)

2 teaspoons lemon juice

Freshly ground black pepper to taste

To make, see Hazelnut & dill pesto (*right*).

Walnut & basil pesto Ⓥ

ready in **2** minutes

30g (1oz) walnuts

A small handful basil (about 5 sprigs)

4 tablespoons olive oil

A drizzle walnut oil

Freshly ground black pepper to taste

To make, see Hazelnut & dill pesto (*right*).

Hemp seed & coriander pesto Ⓥ

ready in **2** minutes

2 tablespoons ground hemp seeds (buy coarsely ground seeds, or use a food blender or coffee/seed grinder)

3 tablespoons olive oil

A small handful fresh coriander (about five sprigs)

½ garlic clove

Freshly ground black pepper to taste

To make, see Hazelnut & dill pesto (*right*).

Pesto prawns

Pesto prawns

cook in `5` **minutes**

(marinade overnight)

8 large raw tiger prawns

3 tablespoons pesto of your choice

Put your chosen pesto in a shallow dish. Add the raw tiger prawns and coat them in the pesto. Leave to marinate for an hour or more.

Soak two wooden skewers in water and thread the tiger prawns onto the soaked skewers. Cook under a medium-hot grill for a couple of minutes on each side and serve.

The pesto prawns can also be left to cool once they have been cooked and eaten cold within 24 hours.

Hazelnut & dill pesto

ready in `2` **minutes**

30g (1oz) hazelnuts

A small handful fresh dill (about 8 sprigs)

4 tablespoons olive oil

2 teaspoons lemon juice

Freshly ground black pepper to taste

The method for all four pestos is very simple and the same for whichever mixture you choose.

Combine all the ingredients in a food processor and whizz together until you have a thick paste. Add more oil if the mixture is too stiff.

To make a smoother paste, zap the seeds (which are harder than the nuts) in a seed or coffee grinder for a few seconds before adding to the food processor.

Pesto dip

ready in `5` **minutes**

50ml (2fl oz) pesto of your choice

100ml (3½fl oz) reduced-fat fromage frais

Selection of raw vegetables such as carrots, peppers, broccoli and cauliflower

Mix your chosen pesto with the fromage frais and pour into a small bowl. Cut the fresh vegetables into thick fingers or chunks.

Use the pesto mix as a dipping sauce for the crudités.

SERVING IDEAS

For lunch Serve the prawns with a few boiled new potatoes and a mixed leaf salad containing fresh coriander.

For dinner For a change, mash some feta cheese with your chosen pesto and spread the mixture on grilled chicken or fish as a topping.

Walnut & basil pesto

Complete salads

These dishes are complete salads because they provide all the protein and complex carbohydrates you need for one meal; there's no need to prepare anything else to eat with them. Use ingredients that are as fresh as possible to give the best taste and flavour. All recipes serve two.

Sweet potato, feta & avocado salad ⓥ

ready in **25** minutes

200g (7oz) sweet potato

1 tablespoon olive oil

1 tablespoon lemon juice

Freshly ground black pepper

1 bunch watercress

10 black olives, pitted

70g (2½oz) feta cheese

½ avocado, peeled

For the dressing:

2 tablespoons orange juice

2 tablespoons lemon juice

1 teaspoon soy sauce

Bake or boil the sweet potato in its skin until just cooked. Depending on its size and shape, this should take 15–20 minutes. Don't overcook the potato or you will end up with a mush. Peel while still warm and cut into 2.5cm (1in) cubes. Put in a bowl, toss with the oil and lemon juice, season with black pepper and leave to one side to cool.

Mix the dressing. Cut the stalks off the watercress, tear the top sprigs into two bowls and toss them in the dressing. Pile the sweet potato onto the leaves and add the olives. Chop the feta cheese and peeled avocado into the same sized chunks, pile on top of the sweet potato and serve.

You can also toast a couple of tablespoons of pinenuts and scatter them over each salad, or add a spoonful of a Food Doctor seed mix for added taste and crunch.

Sweet potato, feta & avocado salad

Winter salad with cashews Ⓥ

ready in **10** minutes

75g (2½oz) peeled celeriac, coarsely grated

50g (2oz) raw unsalted cashew nuts

1 teaspoon caraway seeds

75g (2½oz) red cabbage, finely shredded

1 handful fresh parsley, coarsely chopped

1 tablespoon The Food Doctor Fennel and Caraway Seed Mix, or use ¼ teaspoon fennel seeds mixed with 1 tablespoon mixed pumpkin and sunflower seeds

For the dressing:
3 tablespoons live natural low-fat yoghurt

2 tablespoons lemon juice

1 garlic clove, crushed

Freshly ground black pepper

Put the celeriac in a bowl. Mix the dressing and add it to the bowl. Leave to one side.

Dry-roast the cashews in a dry frying pan and toss frequently to prevent burning. Repeat with the caraway seeds until they pop – it will take just a few seconds.

Combine the cashews and caraway seeds with the celeriac, mixing well. Gently stir in the red cabbage and the fresh parsley. Serve topped with the seed mix.

You can also serve the salad with grilled haloumi cheese on top.

Red rice salad Ⓥ

50g (2oz) Camargue red rice

300ml (½ pint) weak stock

50g (2oz) yellow split peas or split mung beans

3 tablespoons The Food Doctor Rosemary & Garlic Seed Mix, or use 3 tablespoons mixed pumpkin, sesame, sunflower and linseeds with ½ teaspoon garlic, chopped

1 fat spring onion, finely sliced

½ large red pepper, chopped

½ courgette, cut into matchsticks

2 tablespoons fresh mixed herbs, chopped (parsley, coriander, mint, basil, rosemary, marjoram, etc.)

For the dressing:
50ml (2fl oz) olive oil

2 tablespoons lime juice

1 tablespoon soy sauce

Cook the rice in 150ml (¼ pint) stock for 25 minutes (it should be cooked but with a little bite). Drain off any liquid and put in a bowl.

Meanwhile, rinse the split peas and soak them in water for 10 minutes. Drain and simmer in the remaining stock for 10 minutes until they are soft but not collapsing. Tip into the bowl with the rice, add the dressing and allow to cool.

Once cold, add the rest of the ingredients. Mix well and serve.

For a change, use wild rice instead of red rice, but cook it until it explodes so that it is easy to eat. Or try stirring in a couple of tablespoons of sprouted seeds.

Chinese chicken salad

ready in **20** minutes

100g (3½oz) fine noodles (preferably buckwheat)

1 tablespoon sesame oil

150g (5oz) cold chicken meat, coarsely shredded

60g (2oz) beansprouts (either home-sprouted, or ready sprouted from a health food shop or supermarket)

2 spring onions, trimmed and finely sliced lengthways

½ red pepper, finely sliced

¼ green pepper, finely sliced

1 tablespoon sesame seeds

For the dressing:
1 tablespoon soy sauce

2 tablespoons orange juice

1 tablespoon lemon juice

10cm (4in) cube fresh ginger, grated

1 teaspoon balsamic vinegar

1 tablespoon sesame oil

Mix all the ingredients for the dressing together in a jug or bowl.

Cook the noodles according to the instructions on the packet. Once cooked, drain, toss in the sesame oil and allow to cool.

While the noodles cook, prepare the rest of the ingredients and mix them together in a bowl. Pour over the dressing and allow to stand until the noodles are ready. Then toss in the drained, cooled noodles and serve with a crisp green salad.

Chicken & avocado salad

Quinoa is the base for this salad: it's gluten-free and has a low GI rating. Add the chicken and avocado, and this dish becomes a filling and healthy meal that is high in nutrients. Serves two.

ready in 40 minutes

150g (5oz) quinoa

220ml (7fl oz) vegetable or chicken stock *(see p.86)*

1 tablespoon olive oil

Juice 1 lemon

Approx 100g (3½oz) cold chicken, cut into bite-sized chunks

½ avocado

½ red pepper, roughly chopped

70g (2½oz) cucumber, roughly chopped

3 baby courgettes (approx 60g/2oz) cut into chunks

2–3 tablespoons mixed fresh herbs (mint, parsley, coriander and basil, depending on what is available), chopped

Put the quinoa into a medium-sized saucepan and pour in the stock. Bring to the boil and simmer the quinoa in the stock over a medium-low heat until the stock has all absorbed. This should take about 15–20 minutes, by which time the quinoa should be cooked. Stir in the olive oil and the lemon juice and set aside to cool.

Once cool, stir in the rest of the ingredients, divide between two plates and serve.

Remoulade & smoked meat

Remoulade is a French dish that is usually made with mayonnaise. This recipe uses fromage frais instead, which is low in fat and has a good protein content. Remoulade also goes well with smoked mackerel.

ready in 15 minutes

100ml (3½fl oz) live natural low-fat yoghurt

100ml (3½fl oz) reduced-fat fromage frais

2 tablespoons lemon juice

2 tablespoons Dijon mustard

Freshly ground black pepper

175g (6oz) celeriac, finely grated

12 spears asparagus

A drizzle of olive oil

A drizzle of lemon juice

4 slices smoked venison or smoked duck

Combine the yoghurt, fromage frais, lemon juice, mustard, and black pepper in a bowl. Add the celeriac, stir well and leave to stand for about 15 minutes for the flavours to combine.

Meanwhile, steam the asparagus until just tender. This should take approximately 10 minutes. Once cooked, put the asparagus on a plate, drizzle with a little olive oil and lemon juice while still hot and season with freshly ground black pepper.

Divide the asparagus, the remoulade and the smoked meat between two plates and serve. Serve with wholemeal bread or flat bread as a light lunch for two. This dish can also be used as a starter for four people.

Poached egg rosti ⓥ

This is the ideal easy meal to make when you don't have time to cook elaborate meals. If you are feeling hungry, cook two eggs per person and allow a little longer for the cooking time. Serves two.

ready in 25 minutes

300g (10oz) grated sweet potato

300g (10oz) grated celeriac

Zest and juice 1 lemon

1 tablespoon olive oil

2 tablespoons brown mustard seeds

A small bunch fresh dill, finely chopped

2 eggs

Mix the sweet potato and celeriac in a bowl with the lemon juice and zest. Heat the olive oil in a saucepan, add the mustard seeds and cook for a few seconds over a high heat until they pop. Pour the oil and seeds over the grated vegetables. Add the fresh dill and mix all the ingredients together.

Heat a little oil in a frying pan and add the vegetables, patting them down to form a cake. Cook over a medium-high heat for about 10 minutes to allow the underside to colour. Slip the pan under a high grill for another five minutes or so to brown the top.

Keep warm in a medium-hot oven while you poach the eggs *(see p.25)*. Serve the rosti with a poached egg placed on top of each portion.

SERVING IDEAS

For lunch Serve with a side salad and flat bread *(see p.88)*.

For dinner Crumble feta cheese over each egg and serve with a mixed salad.

Cannellini bean stew with tomatoes Ⓥ

If you have time, you can cook dried cannellini beans for a slightly better texture. Soak them according to the instructions on the packet and cook them for approximately 1 hour. This recipe serves two.

| ready in **15** minutes |

1x400g (13oz) can cannellini beans or 200g (7oz) dried beans

8 cherry tomatoes, cut in half

1 teaspoon mixed herbs, dried

200ml (7fl oz) vegetable stock *(see p.86)*

Juice ½ lemon

1 teaspoon mustard

1 tablespoon olive oil

A small handful mixed fresh herbs, chopped, as a garnish

Put all the ingredients into a medium-sized pan, bring to the boil and simmer gently for 15 minutes. When the beans are cooked through, use a fork to gently break them up. Mix the stew well.

Divide the stew between two plates, scatter the chopped fresh herbs on top of each portion and serve.

SERVING IDEAS

For lunch For an instant protein to serve with this stew, use cold chicken pieces from the fridge, ready marinated tofu (available from delicatessens) or some smoked fish.

For dinner If you have time to cook, serve this as a side dish with Stuffed pork fillet *(see p.120),* or grilled chicken or fish.

Use **canned tomatoes** from the **storecupboard** if you don't have any **fresh** tomatoes

Cherry tomatoes have an intense sweet taste that heightens the flavour of cooked dishes such as this Cannellini bean stew.

Three ways with mushrooms

With their characteristic earthy flavour and meaty-tasting juices, mushrooms can sustain and even be enhanced by powerful flavours such as lemon, feta cheese and garlic. These recipes all serve two.

SERVING IDEAS

For lunch Serve the Greek mushroom & feta cheese salad with flat bread or wholemeal bread to soak up the juices.

For dinner Serve the Stuffed mushrooms with a mixed leaf salad or Simple roasted tomatoes *(see p.33)*, or both. Serve the Mushroom bake with a crisp green salad.

Flat bread

Greek mushroom & feta cheese salad

Greek mushroom & feta cheese salad Ⓥ

ready in **25** minutes

12 cherry tomatoes, skinned

8 baby onions or shallots (about the same size as the mushrooms; if bigger, cut in half)

2 tablespoons olive oil

200g (7oz) button mushrooms

100ml (3½fl oz) vegetable stock *(see p.86)*

50ml (2fl oz) white wine

1 bay leaf

2 teaspoons coriander seeds, whole

1 teaspoon black peppercorns, whole

1 tablespoon white wine vinegar

A small handful each fresh coriander and parsley, chopped

100g (3½oz) feta cheese, cubed

To skin the tomatoes, make a small slit in their skins, place in a bowl and pour over boiling water. Drain almost immediately and the skins should slip off. Leave to one side.

Heat the olive oil in a frying pan and gently brown the onions. Continue to cook over a low heat until they soften. Add the mushrooms and stir, then add the stock, white wine, bay leaf, coriander and peppercorns. Bring to the boil and simmer gently for 15 minutes until the onions are cooked. Add the tomatoes and vinegar, turn into a bowl and allow to cool. If you prefer, you can chill the mix in the fridge.

Serve with the feta gently folded into the mixture and the fresh herbs scattered on top.

Mushroom bake Ⓥ

ready in **20** minutes

1 medium aubergine

2 medium courgettes

A drizzle of olive oil

4 large portabello mushrooms

Freshly ground black pepper

2–3 medium tomatoes, sliced

200g (7oz) feta cheese, sliced

A squeeze of lemon juice

4 sprigs fresh rosemary

A handful fresh parsley, coriander and basil, chopped

Preheat the oven to 180°C/350°F/gas mark 4.

Thinly slice the aubergine and courgettes diagonally. Drizzle a little oil over them and brown on a griddle or under a grill.

Arrange the mushrooms in a lightly oiled ovenproof dish. Drizzle a little more olive oil over them and season with black pepper. Arrange 2–3 tomato slices over each mushroom, followed by slices of courgette and aubergine. Top with sliced feta and a squeeze of lemon juice. Tuck the rosemary around the mushrooms, cover with foil and bake for about 30 minutes until the mushrooms are soft.

Serve with the chopped herbs scattered over the top. This dish can also serve four as a starter.

Stuffed mushrooms Ⓥ

ready in **20** minutes

4 flat brown mushrooms, approx 50g (2oz) each

A drizzle of olive oil

Freshly ground black pepper

1 tablespoon olive oil

1 small onion, finely chopped

1 clove garlic, crushed or chopped

50g (2oz) fresh rye breadcrumbs

Zest 1 lemon

2 sprigs fresh sage, finely chopped

2 sprigs fresh thyme, finely chopped

2 tablespoons pinenuts, dry roasted

3 tablespoons The Food Doctor Sage & Thyme Seed Mix, lightly crushed, or use 3 tablespoons mixed pumpkin, sesame and sunflower seeds and ½ teaspoon each dried sage and thyme

60g (2½oz) feta cheese, crumbled

Preheat the oven to 180°C/350°F/gas mark 4.

Lightly oil a shallow ovenproof dish and lay the mushrooms side by side. Drizzle a little olive oil over each and season with black pepper. Cover loosely with foil and bake for 10–15 minutes.

Meanwhile, heat the oil in a frying pan over a low heat, add the onion and cook gently until soft. Add the garlic and bread and stir until the breadcrumbs turn brown and crisp. Add the lemon, sage, thyme, black pepper, pinenuts and seed mix. Mix well and stir in the feta.

Divide the stuffing evenly among the mushrooms, patting it down firmly. Pop under a grill to brown for a few minutes and serve.

Crunchy toppings & fresh dressings for fish

Although easy to prepare, plain cooked fresh fish sometimes needs something a little more exciting to liven up a meal. These toppings and dressings are an instant solution to such a dilemma, and give fish fillets and steaks a delicious flavour and texture. All recipes serve two.

Lemon & spring onion topping

2 oatcakes

1 spring onion coarsely chopped

1 heaped teaspoon poppy seeds

1 teaspoon lemon zest

To make, see right.

Cumin & coriander topping

3 tablespoons The Food Doctor Original Seed mix

½ teaspoon cumin seeds

3 sprigs fresh coriander

To make, see right.

Spiced crunchy topping

2 thin slices rye bread, toasted until fairly crisp

1 teaspoon coriander seeds, dry-roasted over a medium-high heat for 3–4 minutes

¼ teaspoon ground cinnamon

¼ teaspoon ground ginger

To make, see right.

Walnut & citrus zest topping

ready in **1** minutes

20g (½oz) walnuts

1 teaspoon black mustard seeds, dry-roasted over a medium-high heat until the seeds pop

3 sprigs fresh parsley

½ teaspoon orange zest

½ teaspoon lemon zest

To make a topping, put all the ingredients in a food processor. Whizz for 10 seconds for a coarse topping, or up to 30 seconds for a finer texture.

Watercress salsa

ready in **1** minutes

A small handful watercress, with stalks trimmed

1 medium tomato

1 tablespoon lemon juice

1 tablespoon olive oil

½ teaspoon soy sauce

1 small spring onion, trimmed and coarsely chopped

Freshly ground black pepper

Put all the ingredients in a food processor and whizz for a few seconds to give a coarse texture. Turn out into a small bowl and chill in the fridge until you are ready the serve the fish.

Watercress salsa

Hot horseradish dressing

Hot horseradish dressing

ready in **1** minutes

2 tablespoons reduced-fat fromage frais

2 tablespoons live natural low-fat yoghurt

1 tablespoon horseradish sauce (*see pp.150–151*)

Juice and rind 1 lemon

Freshly ground black pepper

A small handful chives, finely chopped

Put all the ingredients in a bowl and mix well. Turn out into a small bowl and chill in the fridge until you are ready to serve the fish.

Crunchy fish fillets

ready in **20** minutes

2x100g (3½oz) fish fillets or steaks (cod, haddock, tuna, swordfish, salmon, etc.)

A drizzle of lemon juice

Freshly ground black pepper

Your choice of crunchy topping

Preheat the oven to 180°C/350°F/gas mark 4.

Place the fillets (skin side up if the skin is still attached) in a lightly oiled, shallow, ovenproof dish. Sprinkle the lemon juice over the fish and season with freshly ground pepper, then turn the fillet over and repeat. Cover the white flesh of the fillet with a generous layer of crunchy topping and press it down gently with your hand.

Cover the dish with foil and bake for 10–15 minutes, depending on the thickness of the fish (it should be slightly underdone when cooked).

When the fish is just cooked, remove the foil, drizzle the topping with a little more olive oil and slip the ovenproof dish under a hot grill for a couple of minutes until the topping is browned and crunchy.

SERVING IDEAS

For lunch Serve with the Watercress salsa and Hot horseradish dressing, a leafy salad and a small serving of brown rice or bulgar wheat.

For dinner Serve with the salsa and horseradish dressing, some steamed green beans or a spoonful of Chick-pea & caramelized onion mash (*see p.33*).

Crunchy fish fillet with Cumin & coriander topping

Stir-fries

The secret of a successful stir-fry is the preparation – cooking is easy. These recipes are high on flavour and low on effort, so they may become firm favourites. All recipes serve two.

SERVING IDEAS

For lunch Serve the Coriander chicken stir-fry with brown or red rice, quinoa or socca. The Pork & spring vegetable stir-fry goes well with buckwheat noodles.

For dinner Omit the rice, quinoa, socca and buckwheat noodles and sprinkle on a tablespoon of toasted mixed seeds (*see pp. 126–127*).

Red rice

Coriander chicken stir-fry

Coriander chicken stir-fry

`ready in 20 minutes`

200g (7oz) chicken breast, finely sliced

1 teaspoon dry-roasted coriander seeds

100g (3½oz) green cabbage, finely sliced

2 tablespoons olive oil

4 tablespoons live natural low-fat yoghurt, flavoured with ½ teaspoon each ground cumin and ground chilli (to taste)

For the marinade:

1 teaspoon ground coriander

2 tablespoons fresh coriander, chopped (reserve a little for a garnish)

2 spring onions, finely sliced

2 teaspoons sesame seeds

3 tablespoons olive oil

Zest 1 orange (reserve a little for a garnish)

2 tablespoons orange juice

2 tablespoons lemon juice

Freshly ground black pepper

Combine the marinade ingredients in a bowl and mix. Add the chicken, stir well and leave to stand.

Heat a small saucepan over a medium-high heat, add the coriander seeds and dry-roast them for 30 seconds until they pop.

Just before cooking, add the roast coriander seeds and shredded cabbage to the chicken.

Heat the oil in a wok and add the chicken mix. Cook over a medium-high heat until the chicken is cooked and the cabbage is wilting (add some water if it appears dry). Stir in the yoghurt and garnish with the orange zest and fresh coriander.

Mixed vegetable & bulgar wheat stir-fry

`ready in 20 minutes`

100g (3½oz) bulgar wheat

100ml (3½fl oz) boiling vegetable stock

100g (3½oz) asparagus stems

75ml (3fl oz) water

2 teaspoons Thai fry paste

1 teaspoon tamarind paste

1 tablespoon dry white wine

1 tablespoon rice wine vinegar

½ teaspoon chilli paste

100g (3½oz) broccoli in small florets

½ red pepper, cut into strips

½ yellow pepper, cut into strips

A drizzle of soy sauce

A drizzle of sesame oil

100g (3½oz) hot smoked fish, smoked tofu or feta cheese

Soak the bulgar wheat in the stock for 15 minutes, by which time it should be plump. Drain and squeeze through a fine sieve.

Heat lightly salted water in a saucepan, add the asparagus, bring to the boil and simmer for a minute or so. Drain and leave to one side.

Combine the water, Thai fry paste, tamarind paste, wine, vinegar and chilli paste in a small jug. Heat a wok, pour in the sauce and bring it to the boil. Toss in the broccoli and peppers, cook for 2 minutes, add the asparagus and stir for another minute. Stir in the bulgar wheat.

Serve with a drizzle of soy sauce and sesame oil, topped with the hot smoked fish, tofu or feta cheese.

Pork & spring vegetable stir-fry

`ready in 20 minutes`

150–200g (5–7oz) pork fillet

1 tablespoon olive oil

50ml (2fl oz) unsweetened apple juice

100g (3½oz) new baby carrots, cut lengthways

2 sticks celery, cut into short strips

50g (2oz) mangetout

1 fat or 2 thin spring onions, cut lengthways into 6cm (2½in) sticks

50g (2oz) broad beans

Freshly ground black pepper

For the marinade:

1 tablespoon soy sauce

2 tablespoons lemon juice

1 teaspoon fresh ginger, grated

1 tablespoon unsweetened apple juice

Trim any fat from the pork and cut it into short strips. Combine all the ingredients for the marinade, add the pork and allow to stand while you prepare the vegetables.

Heat the olive oil in a wok, lift the pork from the marinade and quickly brown the strips. Remove from the wok and put to one side. Pour the apple juice into the wok and add all the vegetables except the broad beans. Stir-fry for 5 minutes or so, return the pork to the wok and add the broad beans and the marinade. Continue to stir-fry for a further 5 minutes until the pork is cooked and the vegetables are al dente, then serve.

Smoked haddock tartare

It's important that you include fish in your diet at least twice a week: fish is both an ideal source of protein and rich in essential fats, which is essential for a healthy metabolism. This recipe is a fast and simple way to ensure that you get your quota. Serves two.

Use unsmoked haddock if **you prefer** a milder **flavour**

Yoghurt dressing Ⓥ

ready in **2** minutes

2 tablespoons live natural low-fat yoghurt

2 tablespoons reduced-fat fromage frais

1 tablespoon lemon juice

1 tablespoon olive oil

Combine all the ingredients in a small bowl or jug and mix together to a mayonnaise consistency.

Keep the dressing chilled in the fridge until the Smoked haddock tartare is ready to be served.

Smoked haddock
tartare with flat bread

Smoked haddock tartare

ready in **5** minutes

200g (7oz) smoked haddock (undyed)

Juice and rind 1 lemon

½ teaspoon Dijon mustard

½ teaspoon capers, finely chopped

A small handful fresh dill, chopped

A small handful fresh chives, chopped

A large bunch fresh watercress, trimmed and tossed in a drizzle each of olive oil and fresh lemon juice

Carefully remove any skin and bones from the haddock. Using a large, sharp knife, cut the fish into thin strips, then chop the strips crosswise very finely to make tiny cubes. Don't be tempted to use a food processor to do this job, as it will leave the fish in a mushy pulp.

Combine the shredded fish with the lemon juice and rind, mustard, capers and the fresh herbs in a bowl and mix the ingredients well. Put the fish to one side while you make the flat breads *(see right)*, or leave to marinate in the fridge for half an hour or so until you are ready to eat.

Once you have made enough flat breads, divide the fresh watercress between two plates and top each pile of watercress with half the haddock mix. Serve with the flat bread on the side and the yoghurt dressing in a small jug or bowl.

This makes a perfect light lunch for two people, or you can use it as a starter for four people.

Yoghurt dressing

Flat bread

ready in **10** minutes

100g (3½oz) chick-pea flour

40ml (2fl oz) olive oil

200ml (7fl oz) water

A small handful fresh coriander, chopped

Zest of 1 lemon

Put the flour into a bowl, make a well in the middle and add the olive oil. Gradually pour in the water, mixing constantly with a whisk, until you have a batter about the consistency of double cream. (The batter shouldn't spread everywhere when poured into a pancake pan.) Add the coriander and lemon zest and stir well.

Heat a non-stick pancake pan until very hot, brush with olive oil and pour in about 100ml (4fl oz) of the batter. The batter should form a thick pancake about 20cm (8in) across. Lower the heat slightly and allow the flat bread to cook and brown before flipping it over and browning it on the other side. Lift out the flat bread, put it on a plate, cover with an upturned plate and keep in a warm oven while you use the rest of the mix.

This recipe should make at least four flat breads. Any excess flat breads can be kept covered in the fridge for up to two days or frozen for up to four weeks.

See page 88 for more flat bread recipes.

Pan-fried seafood

Seafood is a perfect ingredient to use when preparing quick meals, as it only needs a few minutes to cook through. Ensure that the seafood you buy is as fresh as possible. Serves two people.

ready in 15 minutes

200g (7oz) mixed fish (raw prawns, prepared squid, monkfish tail, white fish fillet), cut into bite-sized pieces

1 small cube of ginger, finely grated

Juice ½ lemon

Freshly ground black pepper

100g (3½oz) bulgar wheat, plus boiling water to cover

1 tablespoon olive oil

2 shallots, finely chopped

2 garlic cloves, crushed or finely chopped

A small bunch fresh dill, chopped

For the sauce:

6 tablespoons live natural low-fat yoghurt

Zest and juice 1 lime

Put the fish into a bowl. Toss them in the ginger and lemon juice and add a grinding of black pepper. Leave the fish to marinate for 5 minutes. Mix the sauce ingredients together and decant into a small jug.

Put the bulgar wheat into another bowl and pour over lightly salted boiling water until the bulgar wheat is just covered. Leave to stand for 10 minutes, by which time the bulgar wheat should be plump and soft.

Heat the oil in a frying pan, add the shallots and soften over a low heat. Add the garlic and cook for a few seconds. Lift the fish from the bowl, add it to the pan and cook over a medium-high heat, tossing continually. This shouldn't take more than a couple of minutes. When cooked, drain and squeeze the bulgar wheat through a sieve and add it and the marinating juices to the pan. Add more lemon juice and black pepper if needed and stir in the chopped dill. Serve with the yoghurt and lime sauce on the side.

Hot griddled squid & salsa

The strong, sharp flavours of this salsa contrast well with the lightly spiced squid. Try to buy small or baby squid, as bigger squid can be too thick and become rubbery once cooked. Serves two.

ready in 20 minutes

300g (10oz) squid, cut into rings with the tendrils cut into 5–6cm (2–2½in) lengths

1 teaspoon fresh ginger, grated

Juice 1 lemon

Freshly ground black pepper

100g (4oz) bulgar wheat, plus boiling stock to cover

1 tablespoon olive oil

Rind ½ lemon

1 handful fresh parsley, finely chopped

A drizzle of olive oil

For the salsa:
A handful fresh mixed herbs such as mint, basil and parsley, chopped

1 large spring onion (or three small ones), finely chopped

1 fat garlic clove, crushed

Juice and rind 1 lime

Freshly ground black pepper

Put the squid in a bowl and combine with the ginger, lemon and black pepper. Leave for about 15 minutes.

Meanwhile, soak the bulgar wheat in the stock for 10 minutes, then drain through a sieve and squeeze out any excess stock. Stir in the olive oil, lemon rind and plenty of chopped parsley. Keep the bulgar wheat warm.

To make the salsa, mix the ingredients in a small bowl.

Use a slotted spoon to lift the squid from the marinade onto a lightly oiled, hot griddle over a high heat. Cook for 5–6 minutes, stirring occasionally to allow the squid to turn a golden colour. Serve immediately with the bulgar wheat, a mixed salad and the salsa on the side.

Coconut Thai fish

Fish is the finest of fast foods, and the more gently it is cooked the better. Heat the fish just until the flesh sets so that it retains its flavour and valuable nutrients. This recipe serves two.

ready in 15 minutes

100g (3½oz) corn or buckwheat noodles

2 teaspoons fresh lemongrass, chopped

2 teaspoons Thai fry paste

½ teaspoon ground turmeric

Juice and rind 1 lime

1 heaped teaspoon fresh ginger, grated

50g (2oz) fresh coconut, grated, or use creamed coconut

1 tablespoon olive oil

75g (2½oz) closed cap mushrooms, sliced

200ml (7fl oz) fish stock

200g (7oz) firm white fish fillet (haddock, hake, monkfish tail or halibut, according to what is available)

200g (7oz) pak choi, coarsely shredded

A small bunch fresh coriander or dill, chopped

Cook the noodles according to the instructions. Drain, toss with a little sesame oil and keep warm.

Combine the lemongrass, Thai fry paste, turmeric, lime, ginger and grated coconut in a bowl.

Heat the olive oil in a wok, add the spice mix from the bowl and stir for a minute to release the flavours. Add the mushrooms and stir for a few seconds. Pour in the fish stock, bring to the boil and add the shredded pak choi, stirring well. Add the fish almost immediately and simmer gently for a couple of minutes until the fish is just cooked, taking care not to break it up.

Add the noodles and mix gently. Divide between two plates, top with the coriander or dill and serve.

Fresh coconut has a more superior flavour than creamed coconut. You should be able to buy a whole coconut at a greengrocer or an Asian supermarket. Crack the coconut open with a long sharp knife, scoop out the flesh with a spoon and grate it.

Tuna carpaccio

This unusual way of preparing tuna means that the flavours are sealed in as the fish cooks and the flesh remains moist. Choose one of four crunchy toppings on pages 48–49 to suit your tastes. Serves two.

ready in **20** minutes

2x100g (3½oz) tuna steak

Enough crunchy topping *(see pp.48–49)* to coat the steaks

A drizzle of olive oil

For the croutons:
2 thick slices rye bread

A drizzle of olive oil

1 garlic clove, crushed

Substitute **salmon** if you **prefer,** and ensure that it is as **fresh** as possible

Spread the crunchy topping over the surface of a plate. Brush the tuna all over with olive oil and roll it in the crunchy topping, pressing down lightly to coat it well. Then wrap the tuna tightly in aluminium foil.

Heat a large cast-iron pan, or a stainless steel frying pan with a heavy base, over a very high heat until really hot. Put the wrapped tuna in the pan and press down gently so that it makes good contact with the hot surface. Cook for 3 minutes or so, turning regularly. Remove from the heat and leave to cool in the foil. The tuna should be cooked on the outside and pink on the inside.

Preheat the oven to 180°C/350°F/gas mark 4.

To make the croutons, brush both sides of the bread slices well with olive oil and crushed garlic. Cut the bread into cubes, place on a baking sheet and bake in the oven for about 20 minutes, turning once, until the croutons are well browned and crunchy.

Once the tuna is cold, slice each steak thinly and arrange the slices on a bed of fresh salad leaves and herbs. Scatter the croutons over the top and serve.

Sautéed dishes

The term "sauté" comes from the French word *sauter*, "to jump". By lightly frying food at a high temperature it literally jumps in the pan and remains tender because it cooks so quickly. This is a great way to cook poultry to prevent it becoming tough. All recipes serve two.

Spicy chicken
sauce

SERVING IDEAS

For lunch Serve any of the three dishes with brown or red rice or flat bread *(see p.88)* if you are feeling hungry.

For dinner Serve the Sautéed pigeon and Spicy chicken with Refried yellow peas *(see p.78),* steamed green beans or a mixed salad. The Spicy chicken sauce cools down the fiery chicken and should be added according to taste.

Spicy chicken sauté

Spicy chicken sauté

ready in 10 minutes

2 chicken breasts (approx 100g/3½oz each), cut into strips

2 tablespoons olive oil

2 teaspoons tamarind paste

50ml (2fl oz) water

150g (5oz) spring cabbage, finely shredded

150g (5oz) sweet potato, grated

Freshly ground black pepper

For the sauce:

2 tablespoons reduced-fat fromage frais

2 tablespoons live natural low-fat yoghurt

Juice and rind 1 lime

¼ teaspoon ground cumin

For the marinade:

¼–½ teaspoon hot chilli powder (depending on taste)

1 small cube fresh ginger, grated

1 teaspoon soy sauce

Juice ½ lime

Mix the marinade ingredients, add the chicken and leave to one side while you prepare the vegetables.

Heat the oil in a frying pan over a medium heat, add the chicken strips and sauté quickly until they are cooked and have turned golden.

Combine the tamarind paste and water and pour into a wok. Bring to the boil and toss in the vegetables. Stir-fry until the cabbage has just wilted and the vegetables are hot.

Mix the sauce ingredients and pour into a jug or bowl. Pile the chicken onto the vegetables and serve.

Sautéed Chicken livers

ready in 5 minutes

150g (5oz) chicken livers

1 tablespoon olive oil

1 tablespoon lemon juice

½ teaspoon balsamic vinegar

A small handful fresh parsley, chopped

Freshly ground black pepper

2 generous handfuls mixed leaves with fresh herbs

2 flat breads *(see p.88)*

French dressing to taste

Rinse and clean any stringy or discoloured bits from the chicken livers and pat the livers dry.

Before cooking the livers, which take 2 minutes, make the flat breads if you don't have any ready made in the fridge or freezer.

Heat the olive oil in a frying pan over a medium heat, toss in the chicken livers and brown them for 2 minutes, turning frequently. Remove them from the heat when their outsides are browned and their insides are still pink, or their texture becomes grainy and dry.

Sprinkle the lemon juice, vinegar and parsley over the livers, season with black pepper and stir the ingredients together.

Put one flat bread on each plate and pile the mixed leaves on top. Drizzle with French dressing, top with the chicken livers and serve.

Sautéed pigeon breasts

ready in 20 minutes

2 tablespoons olive oil

200g (7oz) red onions, chopped

1 garlic clove, finely chopped or crushed

100g (3½oz) mushrooms, sliced

4 pigeon breasts

2 teaspoons mushroom ketchup (or sauce)

1 tablespoon orange juice

75ml (3fl oz) dry white wine

Freshly ground black pepper

A small handful fresh parsley, chopped

Heat a tablespoon of olive oil in a frying pan over a low heat, add the onions and soften, then add more olive oil and cook the mushrooms and garlic until the mushrooms are soft and beginning to brown. Transfer to a warmed serving dish using a slatted spoon.

Turn the heat up and brown the pigeon breasts on both sides. Add the mushroom ketchup, juice and wine and stir. Turn the heat down, cover and simmer for 5 minutes until the pigeon breasts are cooked, but still pink in the middle.

Make four three-quarter length slices in each breast, creating a fan shape. Divide the mushroom and onion mix between two plates and top with two pigeon breasts each. Add black pepper and a tablespoon of lemon juice to the sauce in the pan, simmer for a couple of seconds and pour over the breasts. Scatter with parsley and serve.

Meat escalopes

You need to cook with paper-thin pieces of veal or turkey for these recipes. Place the meat between two sheets of greaseproof paper and bang it out with a wooden rolling pin or the back of a large wooden spoon. This also helps to tenderize the meat. Each recipe serves two.

Veal escalope with brown mushrooms

ready in 10 minutes

2 veal escalopes (approx 100g/3½oz each)
1 garlic clove, crushed
Freshly ground black pepper
Juice 1 lemon
2 tablespoons olive oil
1 small onion, chopped
100g (3½oz) brown mushrooms, sliced
50ml (2fl oz) dry white wine
2 tablespoons live natural low-fat yoghurt
A handful fresh parsley, chopped

Lay the meat in a shallow dish, rub the garlic and black pepper into both sides of each escalope and sprinkle with lemon juice. Leave to one side to marinate while you prepare the rest of the dish.

Heat the oil in a shallow pan over a low heat, add the onion and sauté for a few minutes until it begins to soften. Add the mushrooms to the pan and cook gently until they take on colour. Lift out the onions and mushrooms with a slotted spoon and keep them warm in an oven set at a low temperature.

Turn the heat up, lift the escalopes from the marinade and put them in the pan. Brown each side over a medium-high heat – this should take about 2 minutes. Once they have taken on a golden colour, lift them from the pan and put them into a warmed dish. Put the dish into the warm oven.

Pour the wine into the pan and let it bubble for a few seconds. Stir in the marinade, mix the sauce well and bring it to boiling point. Remove the pan from the heat and stir in the yoghurt. Put the pan back over a very low heat, bring to just below boiling point and stir well to combine all the flavours. Stir in the mushroom and onion mix and heat through.

Pour the sauce over the escalopes, scatter with plenty of chopped parsley and serve.

Turkey escalope with shiitake mushrooms

ready in 20 minutes

2 escalopes turkey (approx 100g/3½oz each fillet)
1 garlic clove, crushed
Freshly ground black pepper
Juice 1 lemon
1 small onion, chopped
100g (3½oz) shiitake mushrooms, sliced
2 tablespoons olive oil
50ml (2fl oz) dry white wine
2 tablespoons live natural low-fat yoghurt
A handful fresh dill, chopped

Prepare this recipe by following the same method as for the Veal escalope with mushrooms (*see left*).

Shiitake mushrooms give a stronger flavour than brown mushrooms, and are known to be a good immune booster.

If fresh shiitake mushrooms are unavailable, buy a packet of dried mushrooms: soak 20g (¾oz) in enough boiling water to just cover for 20 minutes. Add the mushroom stock to the frying pan at the same time that you pour in the wine.

Scatter with fresh dill and serve.

Escalopes may sound complicated, but are **easy** to **prepare** and always **popular**

Freshly grated
carrot

SERVING IDEAS

For lunch Serve with a mixed salad
and a small portion of quinoa if you
are feeling hungry.

For dinner Serve with some steamed
broccoli and a freshly grated carrot side
salad or a spoonful of Refried split
yellow peas *(see p.78)*.

Veal escalope
with mushrooms

Slow cook

Make use of time spent at home by trying out these tempting recipes. They are all the more delicious for being cooked slowly.

Beetroot & butter bean soup Ⓥ

Fresh beetroot is full of minerals such as magnesium, iron and folic acid, while the butter beans provide necessary fibre. This soup freezes beautifully for two to three months. Serves two.

2 tablespoons olive oil

1 red onion, chopped

400g (13oz) beetroot, peeled and diced

800ml (1½ pints) vegetable stock *(see p.86)*

1x400g (13oz) can butter beans, rinsed and drained

Juice and zest 1 orange

Juice 1 lemon

Freshly ground black pepper

2 tablespoons live natural low-fat yoghurt

Heat the olive oil in a saucepan over a low heat, soften the onion for 3–4 minutes, then add the beetroot pieces and stir well for a couple of minutes.

Add the hot stock, bring to the boil and simmer for 30–40 minutes until the beetroot is tender. (This will depend on how old the beetroot is.)

Add the butter beans and orange juice and zest and cook for about 10 minutes. Pour the soup into a blender and whizz until smooth. Return to the pan to reheat, add the lemon juice to taste and season with plenty of black pepper.

Serve hot with a tablespoon of yoghurt swirled into each portion of soup.

> **SERVING IDEAS**
>
> **For lunch** Serve each portion with a slice of wholemeal or rye bread.
>
> **For dinner** Add a palmful of mixed pumpkin, sunflower and sesame seeds to each bowl of soup.

Beetroot is a great source of fibre and is high in antioxidants. The younger and smaller the globes, the sweeter and more delicate the flavour. Buy beetroot that have fresh green leaves, undamaged skin and their stalks still attached.

Roast beetroot with haloumi Ⓥ

Slowly roasting beetroot sweetens and enriches its flavour. Haloumi cheese can turn slightly rubbery if it is left to cool for too long, so cook it just before you are ready to eat. Serves two.

SERVING IDEAS

For lunch Serve as a light lunch with wholemeal, rye or flat bread *(see p.88).*

For dinner Serve as a side dish with Fritatta *(see p.81)*

8 small beetroot, preferably organic (approx. 500g/1lb 2oz)

4 tablespoons olive oil

3 sprigs fresh rosemary or 1 teaspoon dried rosemary

4 garlic cloves, unpeeled (just cut off the tip)

1 heaped teaspoon horseradish sauce *(see pp.150–151)*

Juice 1 lemon

Freshly ground black pepper

200g (7oz) light haloumi cheese

2 handfuls mixed green leaves, including watercress and rocket

French dressing to taste

Preheat the oven to 200°C/400°F/gas mark 6.

Scrub the beetroot well. Trim off any leaves and cut each beetroot in half. Put a tablespoon of olive oil in a roasting tray and toss the beetroot in the oil. Scatter the garlic and rosemary around the beetroot, cover the pan loosely with foil and bake for 20–25 minutes.

Remove the foil, turn the beetroot over and bake uncovered for a further 20–25 minutes.

Depending on their size, the beetroot should be cooked, but not mushy. Lift them from the tray and keep warm. Pick out any rosemary twigs, remove the garlic cloves and squeeze the soft centres out of their outer skins and back into the pan. Add the horseradish, remaining olive oil, lemon juice and black pepper and stir well. Keep to one side while the haloumi cooks.

Arrange the washed leaves on a serving plate. Slice the haloumi into thin slices and cook them either in a medium-hot lightly oiled griddle pan or on a rack in the hot oven. Brown the slices (about 3 minutes on each side in the pan, but a little longer in the oven).

Arrange the beetroot on the leaves and the haloumi on top. Drizzle with a little French dressing and serve.

Savoury squashes

With their golden flesh and soft, slightly sweet taste, squashes are rich in nutrients and complex carbohydrates. Winter varieties, such as acorn or butternut squashes, are not restricted to a particular season because they store well, so you should be able to buy them quite easily. All recipes serve two.

Green leaf side salad

Baked squash with mushrooms

SERVING IDEAS

For lunch Serve the Baked squash with a green leaf side salad.

For dinner Serve any of the squash recipes with meat or fish as a vegetable accompaniment. Alternatively, heat a tin of lentils and stir it into the Baked squash to make a hearty stew.

Baked squash with mushrooms

1 small squash (approx 400g/13oz)

50g (2oz) brown or exotic mushrooms, sliced

2 whole garlic cloves

1 teaspoon cumin seeds, coarsely crushed

1 small onion, finely chopped

1 tablespoon olive oil

Juice 1 lemon

A handful fresh mixed herbs (coriander, parsley, chives, etc.), chopped

50g (2oz) crumbled feta cheese

Preheat the oven to 200°C/400°F/ gas mark 6.

Peel and cut the squash into 5cm (2in) cubes. Wipe and slice the mushrooms. Rub the loose skin off the garlic cloves, but don't peel them, just cut off their tips. Put all these ingredients in a bowl together with the cumin seeds, onion and olive oil and toss well.

Lightly oil a shallow baking dish, tip the squash mix into it and spread the ingredients out. Cover the dish with aluminium foil and bake until the squash is soft (about 30 minutes).

Remove the garlic cloves, squeeze the cooked flesh from their skins and stir it into the squash mix. Drizzle the bake with fresh lemon juice, scatter the chopped fresh herbs and crumbled feta cheese on top and serve.

Stuffed squash Ⓥ

2 small acorn squashes

1 tablespoon olive oil

Freshly ground black pepper

1 leek (approx 100g/3½oz), finely sliced

½ teaspoon caraway seeds

100g (3½oz) brown risotto rice

250ml (8fl oz) light vegetable stock

4 tablespoons The Food Doctor Original Seed Mix, or toast 4 tablespoons of your own seeds *(see p.127)*

50g (2oz) hard goat's cheese, grated

Preheat the oven to 200°C/400°F/ gas mark 6.

Cut the bulbous end off each squash (use the leftover flesh for other squash recipes), leaving two ends of squash each weighing 250–300g (8–10oz).

Scoop out the seeds, then use a sharp knife and a spoon to cut out as much flesh as you can, leaving the skin intact. Drizzle olive oil inside each hollowed out squash, season with black pepper and put them on a baking tray in the oven for 30 minutes to soften the skin and remaining flesh.

Soften the leek in the oil in a large saucepan over a low heat. Add the squash and caraway seeds and stir for a few seconds. Add the rice and stir to combine the flavours. Pour in the stock and simmer until the rice is plump and al dente. Add the mixed seeds and black pepper.

Put the mixture into the softened squash shells, sprinkle the goats' cheese on top, slide under a hot grill for 5 minutes and serve.

Squash with quinoa Ⓥ

100g (3½oz) quinoa, plus 250ml (8fl oz) light vegetable stock

1 courgette (approx 100g/3½oz), sliced into 5mm (⅙in) rings

1 tablespoon olive oil

1 small onion, finely sliced

100g (3½oz) firm-fleshed squash, cut into 2cm (¾in) cubes

Juice ½ lemon

Freshly ground black pepper

75ml (3fl oz) vegetable stock

12 cherry tomatoes, cut in half

A small handful fresh tarragon, chopped

Simmer the quinoa in the stock in a saucepan without a lid. After 25 minutes the quinoa should be cooked and all the stock absorbed.

Brush a ridged griddle pan with olive oil and, once hot, brown the courgette slices on both sides. (If you don't have a griddle, cook the courgette slices with the squash.)

Heat the oil in a wok or large frying pan with a lid and soften the onion. Add the squash and the lemon juice and stir for a few seconds. Add the black pepper and the stock, cover and simmer for about 10 minutes. Then add the tomatoes and courgettes and stir well. Lastly, add the quinoa and tarragon. When the quinoa is heated through, serve.

This dish can also be eaten cold with a drizzle of olive oil and balsamic vinegar drizzled on top. Alternatively, add a spoonful of Yellow pepper sauce *(see p.87)*.

Roasted root vegetables ⓥ

Cook these vegetables in a wide, shallow casserole or baking tray so that they roast evenly and turn crisp at the edges. The larger the vegetable chunks, the longer they will take to cook. Serves two.

SERVING IDEAS

For lunch Serve with flat bread for a light lunch.
For dinner Serve as a side dish with the Citrus-baked chicken dish on page 72.

100g (3½oz) leeks, sliced diagonally

100g (3½oz) parsnips

150g (5oz) sweet potato

150g (5oz) celeriac

200g (7oz) red onion, thinly sliced end to end

100g (3½oz) carrot

100g (3½oz) beetroot

4 whole garlic cloves, with skin intact

1 teaspoon caraway seeds

4 tablespoons olive oil

Freshly ground black pepper

1x400g (13oz) can chick-peas, rinsed and drained

A drizzle of lemon juice and olive oil

Preheat the oven to 175°C/340°F/gas mark 4.

Cut all the root vegetables except the onion and leek into even-sized chunks. Put all the vegetables into a large baking tray or casserole dish together with the garlic and caraway seeds. Toss the vegetables in the olive oil to coat them and season with black pepper.

Roast for about an hour, turning occasionally to prevent burning. When the vegetables are almost cooked, fold in the rinsed and drained chick-peas and return to the oven for about 10 minutes.

Before serving, drizzle with a little more olive oil and lemon juice to taste and serve.

Gratin of celeriac, red onion & asparagus ⓥ

Celeriac tastes quite similar to mashed potato when cooked. Combined with the caramelized onions and tangy feta cheese, it makes a delicious main meal or side dish. Quantities are for two.

300g (11oz) celeriac

2 large red onions, quartered and finely sliced

3 tablespoons olive oil

½ teaspoon ground cinnamon

½ teaspoon balsamic vinegar

1 tablespoon fresh lemon juice

12 thin asparagus shoots, with the tough end broken off

Crumbled feta cheese to garnish

A drizzle of olive oil

Freshly ground black pepper

SERVING IDEAS

For lunch Serve with a mixed leaf salad and wholemeal bread.

For dinner Serve with a poached egg on top of each portion, or with grilled fish or meat.

Preheat the oven to 180°C/350°F/gas mark 4.

Peel the celeriac and cut it into slices about 1cm (½in) thick. Line the bottom of a small flan dish with over-lapping layers of the celeriac. Drizzle with olive oil and season with black pepper and cook in the oven for 40 minutes or so.

Heat the oil in a frying pan over a low heat and soften the onions. Add the cinnamon, vinegar and lemon juice and continue cooking slowly to caramelize them. Don't let the onion slices become hard, so add more olive oil to the pan if the contents begin dries up.

Drop the asparagus into boiling water and cook for about 5 minutes, until just al dente.

Cover the celeriac with the caramelized onions and press down. Arrange the asparagus on top and crumble feta over the top. Put the dish under a hot grill for about 5 minutes until the feta cheese starts to brown.

Divide between two plates and serve. If you have individual gratin dishes, you could prepare and cook each helping separately.

Red onions have a sweeter taste than white onions, and lend a more subtle, mellow flavour to dishes.

Red rice dishes

Red rice, also known as Camargue red rice, has a pleasant nutty flavour and a wine-coloured appearance when cooked. It has a medium GI rating and takes less time to cook than brown rice, so it's a useful addition to your storecupboard. Both recipes serve two.

Chicken & red rice with roast tomatoes

75g (2½oz) red rice

4 small chicken thigh fillets, skinned

Juice 1 lemon

1–2 tablespoons dried oregano

Freshly ground black pepper

2 tablespoons olive oil

1 small onion, chopped

2 garlic cloves, finely chopped

4 teaspoons freshly grated ginger

1 tablespoon dry white wine

300ml (½ pint) chicken or vegetable stock (see p.86)

1 teaspoon whole coriander seeds

4 medium tomatoes, cut in quarters

A drizzle of olive oil

Fresh sprigs of marjoram or coriander

Put the red rice in a saucepan and cover with cold water to soak while you prepare the chicken thighs.

Lay the chicken thighs out flat, make a couple of diagonal incisions into (not through) the outer flesh and rub in half the lemon juice, oregano and black pepper. Turn the thighs over and rub in the remaining juice and herbs. Leave for at least 15 minutes.

Heat a tablespoon of olive oil in a frying pan and soften the onion over a low heat. Add the garlic and ginger and heat gently for a few seconds. Add the chicken pieces (and more oil if necessary) and gently brown the chicken on both sides. Pour in the white wine and let it bubble, then add the stock, the drained rice and coriander seeds. Bring to the boil, turn the heat down and cover. Simmer very gently for about 30–35 minutes until the rice is plump and soft. Most of the stock should be absorbed by this time.

About 15 minutes before the end of the cooking time, preheat the oven to 180°C/350°F/gas mark 4.

Put the quartered tomatoes in a small baking dish, drizzle with oil and season with freshly ground black pepper. Toss the tomatoes in the oil to cover them well and roast for 10–15 minutes.

Before serving the chicken and rice, top each portion with some of the tomatoes and torn herbs.

Thai fried rice

125g (4oz) red rice

250ml (8fl oz) light vegetable stock

2 tablespoons olive oil

100g (3½oz) pork fillet, cut into strips

1 small onion, chopped

½ green pepper, finely sliced

½ teaspoon ground cumin

¼ teaspoon chilli paste

2 lime leaves, crushed

1 garlic clove, crushed or chopped

Juice 1 lime

100g (3½oz) cooked prawns

75ml (3fl oz) dry white wine or unsweetened apple juice

Freshly ground black pepper

A small handful fresh coriander, chopped

Cook the rice in the stock for about 30–35 minutes. Drain and reserve.

Heat a tablespoon of olive oil in a wok. Add the pork and cook over a high heat, turning frequently, until the meat is lightly browned (about 5–10 minutes). Lift out the meat and keep it warm.

Add more oil to the wok if necessary and cook the onion and pepper over a low heat until soft. Add the cumin, chilli, lime leaves, garlic and lime juice and stir together for a minute or so. Add the prawns and stir well, then return the pork to the pan, add the wine or apple juice and stir to combine the flavours. Add the rice and season with freshly ground black pepper to taste. Serve garnished with coriander leaves.

These dishes include **complex carbohydrates** so they must be served with some **protein**

SERVING IDEAS

For lunch Both dishes just need a crisp green leaf side salad.

For dinner Serve with some steamed green vegetables if you want a change from a salad. You could also add a tablespoon of live natural low-fat yoghurt or toasted seeds *(see p.127)*.

Crisp green leaf side salad

Chicken & red rice with tomatoes

Citrus-baked chicken

This is a simple way to liven up a simple chicken dish. The strong citrus flavours give the chicken a sharp, slightly sweet taste. Keep any left-over meat in the fridge to eat cold the next day. Serves two.

4 skinned joints of chicken (leg and thigh joined together)
1 tablespoon olive oil
1 large onion, finely sliced

For the marinade:
Juice and zest 1 lemon
Juice and zest 1 lime
Juice and zest 1 orange
Zest ½ grapefruit
1 tablespoon soy sauce
50ml (2fl oz) olive oil
3 or 4 sprigs fresh basil, shredded

Combine all the marinade ingredients in a bowl. Make a couple of slits across the top of the chicken flesh and leave the joints to marinate for a couple of hours, or even overnight.

Preheat the oven to 175°C/340°F/gas mark 4.

Heat a tablespoon of olive oil in a frying pan over a low heat and soften the onion. Add 2 tablespoons of the marinade and allow the onion to caramelize. Arrange the onion slices in the base of a shallow ovenproof dish.

Gently brown the chicken joints on both sides in the frying pan, then lay them on top of the onion, add 2 tablespoons of the marinade, cover and cook in the oven for about half an hour. The chicken should be tender with the juices running clear when pierced with a sharp knife. Lift onto two plates and serve.

SERVING IDEAS

For lunch Serve with bulgar wheat and a salad.

For dinner The strong citrus flavours of this dish go well with the slightly sweet Roast Vegetable side dish on page 68.

Lemons are a fantastic ingredient for flavouring a piece of meat. Lemon juice also tenderizes meat, helping to break down any sinews.

Lamb shank with garlic & rosemary

This dish must be cooked slowly to release all the flavours and reduce the liquid to a rich, dark gravy. You can, if you wish, double the cooking time for a very slow-baked dish. Serves two.

2x175g (6oz) lamb shanks (or 1 lamb shank approx 350g/11½oz)

2 large sprigs rosemary, each broken into 3 or 4 pieces

1 large garlic clove, peeled and cut into thin sticks

1 tablespoon olive oil

8 shallots, peeled (or 1 medium onion, cut into 6)

1 medium/large carrot, cleaned and cut into chunks

250ml (8fl oz) dry white wine

1 bay leaf

2–3 sprigs fresh thyme

3–4 sprigs fresh marjoram

Freshly ground black pepper

250ml (8fl oz) stock

Prepare the lamb shanks by making 6 or 7 small slits in each shank and stuffing the garlic sticks and rosemary sprigs into them. Wrap in kitchen foil and leave overnight to absorb the flavours.

Preheat the oven to 150°C/300°F/gas mark 2 to slow-cook for 3½ hours, or 140°C/275°F/gas mark 1 to cook very slowly for 7 hours.

Heat the oil in a small casserole over a high heat and brown the lamb shanks all over. Tip in the shallots, carrot chunks and white wine and allow to bubble for a few seconds. Tuck in the bay leaf, thyme and marjoram and season with a good grinding of black pepper. Add stock just until the liquid doesn't quite cover the shanks and put the casserole, tightly covered, in the oven.

When the lamb is ready, remove any skin or fat and serve with the stewed vegetables and juices spooned over the top. This dish only needs some steamed broccoli or kale served with it.

So there's nothing to eat in the fridge

Of course there is. These recipes use basic proteins and carbohydrates from the fridge and storecupboard to make tasty meals.

Quinoa & prawn salad

Keep your freezer stocked with frozen peas and
cooked prawns for recipes such as this. The prawns
must be thoroughly defrosted before you eat them,
but they shouldn't take long to thaw. Serves two.

ready in **15** minutes

SERVING IDEAS

For lunch or dinner Depending on what is in
the fridge, serve with a green salad or chopped
tomatoes and scatter some chopped fresh
herbs (if you have any) over each portion to
give some extra flavour.

100g (3½oz) quinoa

200ml (7fl oz) stock

1 tablespoon olive oil

Juice ½ lemon

50g (2oz) frozen prawns, thawed and drained

50g (2oz) frozen peas, cooked and cooled

A small handful mixed fresh herbs, chopped

Simmer the quinoa in the stock until the stock has
absorbed, by which time the quinoa should be soft
and plump. Allow the quinoa to cool.

Stir in the olive oil, some lemon juice (if you have
any), the prawns and the cooled peas, mix well, add
the fresh mixed herbs and serve.

Sardine salad

Sardines are rich in omega-3 fats – one of the essential fats that the body needs in order to function properly. They are also a good source of protein and supply calcium. Serves two.

`ready in` **25** `minutes`

8 dried mushrooms

4 strips of roast pepper from a jar

6 sundried tomatoes

A drizzle of olive oil and lemon juice

1 can sardines in oil, drained

Soak the mushrooms in warm water for 20 minutes. Then drain them and chop them coarsely.

Chop the peppers and sundried tomatoes. Combine with the mushrooms, olive oil and lemon juice (if you have any) to taste. Fold in the sardines, break them up coarsely with a fork and serve.

SERVING IDEAS

For lunch or dinner Serve on flat bread *(see p.88)* or on wholemeal toast. Top with any chopped fresh herbs you may have.

Sardines are commonly available in cans from supermarkets. However, if you can buy them from a delicatessen marinated in olive oil, chillies, lemons or peppers – or marinate them yourself – their flavour will be much improved.

Lentil & bean dishes

Pulses such as chick-peas and lentils are an ideal source of complete protein. Keep a selection of tinned and dried lentils and beans in your storecupboard for recipes such as these – and use your imagination as to what you can find to serve with them. All recipes serve two.

Baked beans Ⓥ

ready in **15** minutes

1 tablespoon olive oil

1 small onion, chopped

1 garlic clove, crushed or finely chopped

1 stick celery, chopped (or use 1 teaspoon celery seed)

1x400g (13oz) can haricot beans, drained and rinsed

1x250g (8oz) can chopped tomatoes

4 teaspoons soy sauce

50ml (2fl oz) unsweetened apple juice

Freshly ground black pepper

Heat the olive oil in a saucepan and soften the onion over a low heat. Add the garlic and the chopped celery (or celery seed) and cook for another minute or two. Tip in the beans, tomatoes, soy sauce and apple juice, and season with black pepper to taste. Stir well and simmer over a reasonably high heat for about 10 minutes until well thickened, then serve.

Chilli chick-peas Ⓥ

ready in **10** minutes

1 tablespoon olive oil

1 small onion, finely chopped

1 tablespoon tomato paste

1 teaspoon curry powder

¼ teaspoon chilli powder

1x400g (13oz) can chick-peas, rinsed and drained

4 sundried tomatoes, cut into strips

Heat the oil in a saucepan and soften the onion over a low heat. Stir in the tomato paste, curry powder and chilli powder and mix well for a few seconds. Stir in the chick-peas and sundried tomatoes and heat the ingredients together until the chick-peas are hot. This is meant to be a dry dish, but add a tablespoon of water to prevent sticking if necessary.

Serve with a squeeze of lemon juice and fresh herbs if you have some.

Refried split yellow peas Ⓥ

ready in **20** minutes

100g (3½oz) dried split yellow peas (or split mung beans)

150ml (¼ pint) weak vegetable stock

2 tablespoons olive oil

1 small onion, chopped

1 teaspoon cumin seeds, dry roasted

Squeeze of lemon juice

Soak the peas or beans for about 10 minutes, or at least rinse very well. Put them in a saucepan, add the stock and simmer until soft but not mushy, which should take 10–15 minutes. Drain and set aside.

Heat the olive oil in a saucepan and soften the onion over a low heat until it turns brown at the edges – this will bring out the sweet flavour of the onion. Add the cumin seeds, stirring for a few seconds. Tip the peas into the mix and stir over a medium heat for 2 minutes so that the peas take on the flavours of the onions and seeds.

Just before serving, stir in a squeeze of lemon juice to taste.

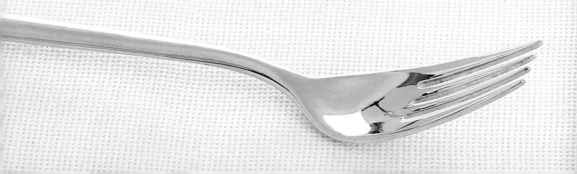

Lemony lentils Ⓥ

ready in 25 minutes

100g (3½oz) puy lentils

1 small onion, finely chopped

¼ unwaxed lemon, finely chopped

1 bay leaf

2 garlic cloves

1 small piece of cinnamon

1 small piece of star anise, about 2 "petals"

400ml (¾pint) water

1 teaspoon soy sauce

2 wedges lemon, to serve

Put all the ingredients except the soy sauce into a saucepan, bring to the boil and simmer gently for about 25 minutes until the lentils are soft but not collapsing. If the mixture looks too watery, raise the temperature slightly and boil away some of the liquid.

Add the soy sauce, stir and serve with a wedge of fresh lemon.

Lemony lentils

SERVING IDEAS

For lunch Serve the Baked beans on toast with a poached egg.

For dinner Serve the Chilli chick-peas with a mixed salad. Serve the Refried split yellow peas with a hard-boiled egg, and the Lemony lentils with 2 tablespoons of mixed seeds.

Lentil stew Ⓥ

Try this storecupboard supper when the fridge holds nothing tempting to eat. Use dried lentils, which only take 10 minutes to cook, or grab a can of lentils instead. Serves two.

25g (¾oz) dried mushrooms

1 small onion, finely chopped

1 tablespoon olive oil

¼ teaspoon cumin seeds

¼ teaspoon turmeric

100g (3½oz) red lentils or 1x200g (7oz) can unsweetened lentils

300ml (½ pint) stock

100g (3½oz) frozen peas

Cover the mushrooms with warm water and soak for about 20 minutes. Then drain and slice them, removing the stems if they seem tough.

Soften the onion in the oil in a medium-sized saucepan over a low heat. Add the spices and cook for a few seconds, then add the lentils and stock and simmer, with the pan covered, for 5 minutes. Add the peas and sliced mushrooms and cook for a further 5 minutes. By this time the stock should be almost absorbed and the lentils soft and starting to collapse. If you use canned lentils, add them with the peas and use just 100ml (3½ fl oz) of stock.

If you have any fresh herbs such as parsley or coriander, chop a good handful into the lentil stew and serve.

SERVING IDEAS

For lunch or dinner You could scatter your favourite Food Doctor seed mix on top of the stew, or use a mixture of pumpkins, linseeds and sunflower seeds.

If you have the right ingredients in the fridge, make a side salad to serve with the stew.

Lentils, which come in various colours, are a nutritionally superior form of vegetable protein. They also contain high levels of fibre and folic acid.

Simple fritatta Ⓥ

This quick and easy dish is so versatile that you can add any fillings you find: canned vegetables or pulses, frozen prawns or peas, roast peppers or artichokes from a jar or sundried tomatoes. Serves two.

ready in 5 minutes

4 eggs

3 tablespoons live natural low-fat yoghurt

1 teaspoon Dijon mustard

Freshly ground black pepper

1 onion, chopped

1 tablespoon olive oil

Fresh herbs (if you have any)

> ### SERVING IDEAS
> **For lunch or dinner** If you have any leftover Roasted root vegetables *(see p.68)*, serve those with the fritatta, or add a handful of fresh herbs. Alternatively, serve with flat bread *(see p.88)*.

Beat the eggs, yoghurt and mustard together in a bowl and season with freshly ground black pepper.

Soften the onion in the olive oil in an omelette pan over a low heat. Pour in the egg mixture. Scatter in whatever filling you have to hand and cook gently to set and brown the bottom. Slip under a warm grill to brown the top and then serve.

Egg pilau ⓥ

Pilau is usually made with rice, but this recipe uses bulgar wheat, which has a lower GI rating than rice. If you don't have any eggs in the fridge, try using tofu or even leftover cold chicken pieces. Serves two.

ready in **15** minutes

SERVING IDEAS

For lunch or dinner Add a handful of chopped fresh parsley and some frozen peas, if you have them, to add colour and flavour to the egg pilau.

100g (3½oz) bulgar wheat, plus enough hot stock to cover

2 tablespoons olive oil

3 tablespoons Dijon mustard

Lemon juice to taste

8 sundried tomatoes

2–3 hard-boiled eggs

Cover the bulgar wheat with boiling stock and leave it to stand for 10 minutes until soft. Drain and squeeze the grains through a fine sieve. Then stir in the olive oil, mustard and some lemon juice if you have any.

Drain the pieces of sundried tomato from a jar, slice them and toss them into the bulgar wheat. Pile the mixture onto two plates, arrange the quartered hard-boiled eggs on top and serve.

Spicy red rice & corn Ⓥ

Red rice is a superior-quality unmilled short-grain rice, so it's slightly sticky when cooked. If you don't have red rice though, you can use brown. Buy cans of sweetcorn without sugar or salt. Serves two.

1 tablespoon olive oil

2 whole cloves

2 cardamom pods (split)

1 small stick cinnamon

1 small onion, finely chopped

100g (3½oz) red rice

300ml (½ pint) stock

1 small can sweetcorn, drained and rinsed

Chopped fresh herbs (if you have any)

Heat the oil in a saucepan over a medium heat and add the spices. Cook for a couple of minutes before adding the onion. Soften the onion over a low heat and allow it to take a little colour, then add the rice and stir into the oil for a few seconds. Add the stock, bring to the boil and simmer gently for 35 minutes until the rice is cooked, but not soggy, and the stock is absorbed. Stir in the sweetcorn, cook over a low heat for 5 minutes to combine the flavours and serve with a garnish of herbs.

SERVING IDEAS

For lunch or dinner Lightly steam some vegetables or prepare a side salad to serve with the rice and sweetcorn if you have any suitable ingredients in the fridge.

Cook now, eat later

These recipes are ideal for preparing in advance. They store well in the fridge or freezer, allowing the flavours to improve.

Stocks & sauces

Many of the recipes in this book require stocks or sauces. If you cook your own stocks – and freeze them in small portions – you'll find that they'll give your food a delicious depth of flavour. The sauces can also be frozen for up to three months or kept in the fridge for three days.

Chicken stock

1 chicken carcass, left over from pot-roasting *(see p.109),* or ask your butcher for 500g–1kg (1–2lb) chicken bits for stock

1 large carrot, scraped and chopped

1 large stick celery

1 large onion

3 sprigs fresh parsley

6 whole peppercorns

A sparse teaspoon sea salt or Lo salt

Remove any remaining meat from the chicken carcass and use for the Chinese chicken salad on page 41, or the Chicken & avocado salad on page 42.

Put the all the bones and skin of the chicken into a large saucepan and add the remaining ingredients (including any onions and lemons that may be left over from roasting). Cover with cold water and bring to the boil. Lower the heat and simmer for at least 2 hours. Then turn off the heat and allow to cool.

Strain the stock and discard all the vegetables and bones. Allow the liquid to stand, then scoop any excess fat off the top of the stock with a spoon or ladle. Return the liquid to the saucepan and boil for about 10 minutes to give the stock a stronger taste.

Use the stock for any recipes in this book requiring bouillon or stock, or use to make a delicious and simple Chicken soup *(see p.93).*

Vegetable stock (v)

2 medium carrots, trimmed and cut into chunks

3 sticks celery, cut into chunks

1 medium onion, quartered

½ small cabbage, coarsely shredded

2 garlic cloves, peeled and coarsely chopped

2 sprigs parsley

6 peppercorns

2 tablespoons soy sauce

2 litres (3½ pints) water

Put all the ingredients into a large saucepan, bring to the boil and simmer over a low heat for an hour and a half. Strain the liquid, adjust the seasoning and use.

Carrots are a great base for stocks. For the best flavour, choose firm young carrots, preferably organic, with their leaves still attached.

Rich tomato sauce ⓥ

2 tablespoons olive oil

1 medium onion, finely chopped

1 medium carrot, finely chopped

1 stick celery, finely chopped

2 garlic cloves, chopped or crushed

2x400g (13oz) cans chopped tomatoes

1 teaspoon tamarind paste

750ml (1¼ pints) dry white wine

2 teaspoons dried mixed herbs

Freshly ground black pepper

2 tablespoons fresh parsley, chopped

Heat the oil in a large saucepan and add the onion, carrot and celery. Soften for about 10 minutes over a low heat, then add the garlic. Raise the heat and cook for a further 5 minutes to intensify the flavours.

Add the tomatoes and tamarind paste, stir well and cook for a further 5 minutes.

Pour in the white wine and allow to bubble for a couple of minutes. Stir in the dried herbs and season with freshly ground black pepper.

Lower the heat, cover the pan and simmer gently for 20 minutes, stirring occasionally.

Once cooked, stir in the fresh parsley. The sauce should be quite thick and rich.

Use the sauce as the base for a balanced soup (just add stock and a can of cannellini or barlotti beans). It can also be blended to make a smoother soup, or served with chunky vegetables. Use as a sauce for the Stuffed gem squash *(see p.108)*, or to accompany the Mixed nut & haloumi roast *(see p.89)*.

Yellow pepper sauce ⓥ

1 large yellow pepper

2 tablespoon olive oil

Juice ½ lemon

½ teaspoon soy sauce

A small handful chives, chopped

Freshly ground black pepper

A splash Tabasco sauce

Preheat the oven to 200°C/400°F/gas mark 6.

Cut the pepper in half lengthways, deseed it and cut each half into three thick strips. Put on a baking tray and drizzle with the olive oil. Put in a hot oven and bake for 30 minutes, turning once.

Tip the peppers and any juices into a food processor together with the rest of the ingredients. Whizz to make a smooth, thick sauce.

For a quicker version, buy a jar of marinated roast peppers, drain and use instead. Serve the sauce with Squash with quinoa *(see p.67)* and Baked trout *(see p.107)*.

Flat breads Ⓥ

These yeast-free breads are a cross between a pitta bread and a pancake. The quantities listed are enough for two people, but you can make more and keep them for up to four weeks in the freezer.

Fennel & caraway buckwheat bread

ready in **10** minutes

100g (3½oz) buckwheat flour

3 tablespoons The Food Doctor Fennel & Caraway Seed Mix, finely ground, or grind 1 tablespoon each pumpkin, sunflower and sesame seeds, ½ teaspoon caraway seeds and ½ teaspoon fennel seeds

40ml (2fl oz) olive oil

200ml (7fl oz) water

Chilli & garlic gram bread

ready in **10** minutes

100g (3½oz) chick-pea flour

3 tablespoons The Food Doctor Garlic & Chilli Seed Mix, finely ground, or grind 1 teaspoon chilli flakes, 1 garlic clove, crushed, 1 tablespoon each pumpkin, sunflower and sesame seeds

40ml (2fl oz) olive oil

200ml (7fl oz) water

To make either, put the flour and ground seeds in a bowl, make a well in the middle and add the olive oil. Gradually pour in the water, mixing with a whisk, until you have a thick batter the consistency of double cream. (The batter needs to be poured into a pancake pan without spreading everywhere.)

Heat a pancake pan until very hot, brush with olive oil and pour in approximately 100ml (4fl oz) of the batter. This should make a thick pancake about 20cm (8in) across. Lower the heat slightly and allow the flat bread to brown before turning and browning the other side. Lift out, cover and keep warm while you finish cooking the rest of the batter.

If you want to add extra flavour to these breads, add some chopped fresh mixed herbs to the batter.

Mixed nut & haloumi roast Ⓥ

The high nut content of this dish makes it rich in omega-6 fats, which are vital for good health. You can prepare the raw ingredients in advance and cook the dish later. It's also good served cold. Serves two.

ready in 5 minutes

150g (5oz) raw unsalted mixed nuts

1 small onion, peeled and quartered

75g (2½oz) mushrooms, quartered

50g (2oz) oat flakes or quinoa flakes

1 tablespoon sesame seeds

2 heaped tablespoons mixed dried herbs

2 tablespoons fresh parsley, chopped

1 large egg, lightly beaten with a fork

1 tablespoon mustard (or 1 teaspoon powdered mustard)

Juice 1 lemon

Freshly ground black pepper

150g (5oz) haloumi cheese, sliced approx 3 mm (⅛in) thick

Preheat the oven to 180°C/350°F/gas mark 4.

Put the nuts, onion and mushrooms into a food processor and whizz together until the nuts are coarsely chopped. Tip the contents into a bowl and add the oat flakes or quinoa, sesame seeds, dried herbs and fresh parsley, stirring well. Add the beaten egg, mustard and lemon juice and season with black pepper.

Lightly oil a 14cm x 20cm (5½ x 8in) oblong loaf tin. Press half the mixture into the bottom of the tin, lay the haloumi slices over the nut mix, cover with the rest of the mix and press down gently. Cover the loaf tin with foil and bake for 45 minutes.

When the dish is ready to be eaten, heat up some Rich tomato sauce *(see p.87)*, cut the nut roast into slices and serve it with the sauce and some steamed broccoli.

Choose nuts that are raw and unsalted for your cooking. Ideal choices are almonds, walnuts, a few Brazil nuts, cashew nuts, pinenuts and hazelnuts.

Stir-fried red cabbage ⓥ

This recipe is a new take on the traditional baked red cabbage and apple, and it's much quicker to make. It will keep covered in the fridge for up to three days. Serves two as a side dish.

ready in **20** minutes

1 tablespoon olive oil

400g (13oz) red cabbage, very finely sliced

1 medium onion, finely sliced

2 tablespoons cider vinegar

Zest and segments 1 orange

3 cardamom pods – crack open and scrape out the seeds

1 garlic clove, crushed or finely chopped

Heat the oil in a wok or a large frying pan. Add the sliced cabbage and onion and toss them in the oil for a minute or two. Add the vinegar, orange zest and segments, cardamom seeds and garlic. Cook for about 20 minutes, stirring frequently. The cabbage should be just a little crunchy and the onion well cooked.

This dish can be served either with grilled meat (especially game) or as a balanced main dish with feta cheese crumbled over it and with a slice of rye bread.

Houmous

This delicious Mediterranean dip is ideal as a snack, since it's high in protein, is filling and versatile. Quantities listed here should be enough for eight snacks. Will keep in the fridge for a week.

1x400g (13oz) can chick-peas, rinsed and drained
2 garlic cloves
3 tablespoons lemon juice
3 tablespoons olive oil
2 tablespoons sesame oil
2 tablespoons soy sauce
Freshly ground black pepper

Put all the ingredients in a food processor and blitz together until smooth. Add more pepper, soy or lemon juice to taste. For an interesting texture, you could stir in 1 tablespoon of toasted sesame seeds. This makes a very light houmous; if you like something heavier, add 1 or 2 tablespoons of tahini.

Serve in a small bowl, with a little olive oil drizzled on top and a sprinkling of chilli powder. Eat it with crudités, spread it on 2 oatcakes, or arrange some green leaves on a flat bread and spread the houmous over the top (add an anchovy fillet too if you like a strong-tasting snack).

Chicken dishes for every occasion

With its high protein content and versatility, chicken is an ideal lean meat to use for cooking healthy meals. These recipes use cheaper cuts of chicken meat to make deliciously tasty dishes that you can serve for a variety of occasions. Each recipe serves two.

Three-grain
wheatfree bread

Sliced chicken terrine,
with caperberries and
chopped tomatoes

Chicken terrine

500g (1lb) chicken thigh fillets (which are moister than breast meat)

Rind 1 lemon

2 large spring onions, cut into chunks

2 teaspoons soy sauce

2 teaspoons grated nutmeg

2 teaspoons olive oil

4 tablespoons reduced-fat fromage frais

Freshly ground black pepper

2 good handfuls mixed fresh herbs (including a little fresh sage), chopped

2 tablespoons olive oil

2 garlic cloves, crushed

400g (13oz) spinach, cut into shreds

Preheat the oven to 150°C/300°F/gas mark 2.

Put the chicken, lemon rind and spring onions into a food processor and blitz until they are well minced.

Combine the mince, soy sauce, nutmeg, olive oil and fromage frais in a bowl. Season with black pepper and fresh herbs. Leave to stand while you prepare the spinach.

Heat the oil in a wok, add the garlic and soften over a medium heat. Add the spinach. When it wilts, drain.

Lightly oil a terrine, add the mince and spinach in layers, cover with foil and bake for 1 hour until the juices are clear. Drain the juices and grill for 5 minutes to brown. Cover with a layer of foil and press down the mix using weights or cans. Leave to cool, draining off any more juice.

Can be kept in the fridge for 3–4 days, or frozen for 4 weeks.

Chicken liver paté

2 tablespoons olive oil

120g (4oz) brown mushrooms, chopped

250g (8oz) chicken livers (organic livers are best) with any stringy or discoloured bits cut off

3–4 large sprigs fresh parsley, chopped

3 sprigs fresh thyme, chopped (or ½ teaspoon dried thyme)

1 teaspoon red wine vinegar

½ teaspoon balsamic vinegar

1 teaspoon soy sauce

1 teaspoon mustard

1 teaspoon lemon juice

Freshly ground black pepper

Heat a tablespoon of olive oil in a frying pan and cook the mushrooms over a medium heat, browning them just a little to bring out the flavour. Tip the cooked mushrooms into a food processor or blender.

Heat the rest of the olive oil in the pan, gently sauté the livers for about 2 minutes on each side (don't overcook them: they should be just pink inside). Remove with a slotted spoon and add to the mushrooms, together with the parsley and thyme.

Add the vinegars, soy sauce, mustard lemon juice and black pepper to the juices in the pan and simmer for 2 seconds. Add to the blender.

Whizz the ingredients for a few seconds. Scrape into a pot and cover.

Store in the fridge for up to three days, or freeze for up to a month if the livers were not previously frozen.

Spring chicken

4 small chicken thighs

1 tablespoon olive oil

12 shallots

50g (2oz) small brown mushrooms

10 cherry tomatoes

3 stems celery, cut into short sticks

100g (3½oz) baby carrots

100g (3½oz) broad beans

50ml (2fl oz) dry white wine

200ml (7fl oz) chicken stock *(see p.86)*

Preheat the oven to 150°C/300°F/gas mark 2.

Skin the chicken thighs and cut away any fat. Put them in an ovenproof casserole. Heat the oil in a frying pan over a high heat and brown each of the vegetables in turn, adding them to the chicken as you go (except the broad beans). Pour the wine into the hot pan, let it bubble for a couple of seconds and add to the casserole. Add the stock, the black pepper and the fresh herbs and cover tightly.

Cook for 1¼ hours, stirring a couple of times. Add the broad beans 15 minutes before the end of the cooking time. The meat should be well cooked and coming away from the bone.

This stew can be refrigerated and reheated the next day or frozen for up to one month.

Simple chicken soup

60g (2oz) brown Basmati rice

50g (2oz) reserved cold chicken meat

1 litre (1¾ pints) chicken stock, plus extra to cook the rice

1 tablespoon lemon juice

1 generous tablespoon fresh parsley, chopped

Freshly ground black pepper

Cook the rice according to the instructions on the packet using the extra chicken stock (rather than water). This should take about 20 minutes to cook.

Meanwhile, shred the cold chicken into smallish pieces. Put the stock into a bowl and add the chicken pieces. Once the rice has cooked, add it and any remaining fluid to the stock, together with the lemon juice. Stir in the parsley and season with black pepper.

This will make approximately 1 litre (1¾ pints) of soup that can be refrigerated for two days, or frozen for up to four weeks. When you come to eat the soup, heat it until just simmering and serve.

Moroccan beef

This delicious dish is full of warm, spicy flavours and beefy juices. It can be refrigerated and reheated the next day – or double-up the quantities and freeze the portions for up to four weeks. Serves two.

400–500g (13–1lb) very lean beef, trimmed and cubed

½ teaspoon each ground cinnamon, ground coriander, ground ginger and ground cumin

2 tablespoons olive oil

1 onion, chopped

2 garlic cloves, finely chopped or crushed

1x400g (13oz) can chopped tomatoes

16 prunes

150g (5oz) broad beans (shelled weight)

A small handful fresh coriander, chopped

2 tablespoons The Food Doctor Original Seed Mix, or 2 tablespoons toasted sesame seeds *(see p.127)*

Preheat the oven to 160°C/320°F/gas mark 3.

Put the beef in a bowl and toss in the ground spices to coat the meat. Leave for a few minutes, then heat a tablespoon of the olive oil in a pan and gently brown the beef in small amounts at a time over a high heat. Once browned, lift the beef out of the pan and into a casserole dish.

Heat the remaining oil in the pan and add the onion, softening it over a low heat. Once the onion is softened, add the garlic. Cook together for a minute or so, then pour in the tomatoes and stir the ingredients together. Pour the mixture over the beef pieces and stir in the prunes. Cook in the oven for 30 minutes.

After half an hour, remove the casserole from the oven and add the beans. Stir them in and add a little stock if necessary. Replace the dish in the oven and cook for a further 30 minutes.

When you come to serve the stew, stir in the fresh coriander, sprinkle the seeds on top and eat with bulgar wheat or brown rice and a green salad.

Normandy pheasant

Pheasant is a rich-tasting but lean meat, so it's a good choice of protein. A hen pheasant is an ideal size to serve two. The dish can be refrigerated and eaten hot the next day, or frozen for up to one month.

1 prepared jointed pheasant (or 2 pheasant breasts)

½ tablespoon cider vinegar

1 tablespoon unsweetened apple juice

1 garlic clove

1 tablespoon olive oil

1 small onion, finely sliced

1 medium-sized cooking apple, peeled, cored and sliced

½ tablespoon calvados or brandy (optional)

50ml (2fl oz) stock

Put the pheasant in a bowl together with the vinegar, apple juice and garlic and marinate it for at least 15 minutes, or preferably an hour.

Heat the olive oil in a saucepan, lift the pheasant from the marinade (which you should reserve) and gently brown the outside of the bird. Once browned, lift the pheasant from the pan and keep it to one side.

Heat the remaining oil in the pan and add the onion. When it starts to soften, add the apple slices. Cook together for 5–10 minutes until the apple starts to soften too, and then replace the pheasant. Pour over

the calvados or brandy and set alight, shaking the pan around while the spirit burns off. Then add the marinade and the stock to the pan and season with a good grinding of freshly ground black pepper.

Bring to the boil, lower the heat and cook over a very gentle heat for approximately 45 minutes, by which time the meat should be tender.

Lightly steam some green vegetables or arrange a salad of crisp mixed leaves when you are ready to serve the dish. If you are eating the pheasant for lunch, you can also add a portion of brown rice or bulgar wheat.

Stews & casseroles

Whether you want to take the strain out of cooking on the night of a special dinner, or stock the freezer with balanced nutritious meals, all these recipes are adaptable enough to be cooked, chilled and reheated the next day or frozen for up to one month. Each recipe serves four.

Pork and beans

400g (13oz) lean pork (leg or fillet) cut into cubes

2 tablespoons olive oil

1 large onion, finely chopped

2 garlic cloves, finely chopped or crushed

1x400g (13oz) can chopped tomatoes

1x400g (13oz) can haricot beans, drained and rinsed

1 green pepper, deseeded and chopped

100ml (3½fl oz) apple juice

2 teaspoons soy sauce

3 sprigs fresh sage, chopped

Freshly ground black pepper

Preheat the oven to 160°C/320°F/gas mark 3.

Heat the oil in a frying pan, and sauté the meat over a high heat, a few cubes at a time, until lightly browned. Remove from the pan and put into a casserole.

Add the onion to the pan and soften over a low heat. Toss in the garlic and cook for 2 minutes more. Tip into the casserole.

Add the tomatoes, beans, green pepper, apple juice, soy sauce and sage to the casserole and season with black pepper. Mix well.

Cover the casserole and cook in the oven for about 45 minutes or until the meat is tender.

Beef goulash

400–500g (13oz–1lb) very lean beef, trimmed and cubed

2 teaspoons paprika (smoked paprika gives a lovely flavour)

2 teaspoons caraway seeds

2 tablespoons olive oil

1 onion, finely sliced

1x400g (13oz) can tomatoes

150g (5oz) sweet potato, peeled and cubed

150g (5oz) celeriac, peeled and cubed

1 bay leaf

200ml (7fl oz) stock

2 tablespoons live natural low-fat yoghurt

Preheat the oven to 160°C/320°F/gas mark 3.

Put the beef, paprika and caraway seeds in a bowl and toss together.

Heat a tablespoon of oil in a frying pan over a high heat and brown the beef, a few cubes at a time. Lift out and put in a casserole.

Heat the remaining oil in the pan and soften the onion over a low heat. Stir in the tomatoes, sweet potato and celeriac. Add to the beef with the stock and bay leaf.

Cook for 1 hour in the oven. Stir a couple of times and check if the stock level needs topping up.

Add the yoghurt just before serving.

Chick-pea stew

2 medium courgettes

2 tablespoons olive oil

1 medium onion, finely sliced

2 garlic cloves, crushed or finely chopped

2 large sticks celery, sliced

1x400g (13oz) can chick-peas, drained and rinsed

1x400g (13oz) can tomatoes

75g (2½oz) green beans, topped and tailed and cut in half

1 bay leaf

Freshly ground black pepper

2 tablespoons The Food Doctor Chilli Seed Mix, coarsely ground, or use ¼ teaspoon chilli flakes and 2 tablespoons mixed pumpkin and sunflower seeds

A large handful fresh parsley or coriander, chopped

Preheat the oven to 180°C/350°F/gas mark 4.

Cut the courgettes in half and slice them lengthways into fairly thick slices. Brush each slice with olive oil and brown under a medium-hot grill or on a ridged griddle pan.

Heat a tablespoon of olive oil in a frying pan and soften the onions. Add the garlic and celery and cook together for a minute or so. Add the chick-peas, tomatoes, beans, courgettes, bay leaf and black pepper. Cook for 2 minutes, then put all the ingredients in an ovenproof casserole and cook for 30 minutes.

Add the seeds and herbs just before you are ready to serve the stew.

Venison stew

2 tablespoons chick-pea flour

400–500g (13oz–1lb) stewing venison, trimmed and cubed

2 tablespoons olive oil

12 shallots

1 tablespoon red wine

300ml (½ pint) stock

½ teaspoon ground nutmeg

2 whole cloves

1 small stick cinnamon

A pinch cayenne

Freshly ground black pepper

8 juniper berries, lightly crushed

A handful fresh parsley, chopped

Preheat the oven to 160°C/320°F/gas mark 3.

Sprinkle the chick-pea flour onto a plate and lightly coat the cubes of meat in the flour.

Heat a tablespoon of olive oil in a frying pan and, once the pan is hot, lightly brown the venison, a few cubes at a time. Lift out the browned pieces of meat and put them into a casserole dish.

Heat the remaining oil and lightly brown the shallots over a medium heat. Lift them out and add them to the venison in the casserole.

Pour the red wine and the stock into the frying pan and stir well to mix them in with the pan juices. Bring to the boil and then pour into the casserole.

Add the spices and juniper berries to the stew, combine well, and cook in the oven for about 1½ hours, by which time the meat should be tender and nearly breaking up.

When you come to serve the stew, scatter the fresh parsley over the top of the dish.

Venison stew

Family food

These healthy recipes are designed to be enjoyed by the whole family. Adapt any ingredients to suit your family's tastes.

Beef carpaccio

Carpaccio, an Italian hors d'oeuvre consisting of paper-thin sliced meat or fish, is usually served raw. This lightly cooked version served with croutons means that the whole family should enjoy eating it.

100g (3½oz) beef fillet per person

1 tablespoon ground The Food Doctor Garlic & Chilli Seed Mix per person, or use 1 teaspoon chilli flakes, 1 crushed garlic clove and 1 tablespoon mixed pumpkin and sunflower seeds per person

1 tablespoon olive oil

For the croutons:
1 slice of rye bread per person

1 tablespoon olive oil

Brush the beef all over with olive oil and then roll the meat in the ground seeds, pressing them well into the meat. Wrap the beef fillets tightly in aluminium foil.

Place a large cast iron pan over a very high heat until really hot. Put the wrapped beef into the pan and press it down lightly so that it makes good contact with the hot surface. Cook for a minute, turning a couple of times. The beef should be cooked on the outside and very pink on the inside when you remove it from the heat. Put the beef, still wrapped in the foil, in the fridge and leave it to cool.

Preheat the oven to 180°C/350°F/gas mark 4.

Cut a thick slice of rye bread per person and brush both sides well with olive oil and crushed garlic. Cut the bread into cubes, place on a baking sheet and bake for approximately 20 minutes, turning once. They should be well browned and crunchy.

Wait until the beef is very cold before serving it because it will be easier to slice. Slice each fillet as thinly as possible using a long, very sharp knife.

> ### SERVING IDEAS
> **For lunch or dinner**
> Serve the thinly sliced beef on a bed of fresh salad leaves and mixed herbs, with some of the rye bread croutons scattered over the top.

Three-bean soup

This robust soup is a great way of getting the family to eat more pulses (such as flageolet beans), which are inexpensive, are high in protein and fibre and carry a low GI rating. This recipe serves four.

ready in **15** minutes

1 tablespoon olive oil

2 shallots, finely sliced

1 garlic clove, finely chopped

100g (3½oz) green beans, topped and tailed and cut in three

1 litre (1¾ pints) hot vegetable stock *(see p.86)*

200ml (7fl oz) tomato passata (cooked tomato concentrate)

100g (3½oz) broad beans (weight after shelling – or use frozen)

1x400g (13oz) can flageolet beans

Juice 1 lemon

Freshly ground black pepper

2 tablespoons mustard

2 spring onions, finely chopped

2 tablespoons fresh parsley, chopped

Heat the oil in a large saucepan, add the shallots and soften them over a low heat. Add the garlic and green beans and stir together for a minute. Pour in the hot stock and passata and simmer for 5 minutes until the green beans are nearly tender. Add the broad beans, the flageolet beans and lemon juice and season with freshly ground black pepper. Simmer for a further 5 minutes.

Stir in the mustard and serve immediately, topped with the spring onions and chopped parsley.

SERVING IDEAS

For lunch Serve each portion of soup with a fresh wholemeal roll.

For dinner Add a tablespoon of live natural low-fat yoghurt to each bowl of soup and sprinkle a generous tablespoon of toasted mixed seeds on top *(see p.127)*.

Smoked fish & sweet potato cakes

Sweet potato may not seem an obvious ingredient for a fishcake recipe, but it packs a lot of nutrition into a single meal and is especially easy to digest. This recipe serves four.

4 sweet potatoes (150–200g/5–7oz each)

4 tablespoons lemon juice

400g (13oz) hot smoked fish (trout, mackerel or salmon)

2 teaspoons fish sauce

8 tablespoons fresh parsley, finely chopped

A little olive oil

4 lemon wedges

Boil the sweet potato whole in very lightly salted water until soft for about 25 minutes. Remove from the water, peel and mash in a bowl together with the lemon juice. Flake in the fish, the fish sauce and the parsley and stir gently to combine the ingredients.

Divide the mixture into 16 small cakes. Heat a little oil in a non-stick frying pan and brown the cakes on both sides, turning only once. Serve with a wedge of lemon at the side of each plate.

This meal can also serve eight as a starter.

> ### SERVING IDEAS
> **For lunch** This meal is quite filling and should only need a mixed salad, but if you are feeling hungry add a serving of quinoa.
>
> **For dinner** Serve with a large salad of mixed leaves and some sliced tomato on the side.

The **tang** of smoked fish combines **beautifully** with the **milder flavour** of sweet potato to make a **delicious** main course

Sweet potatoes contain a variety of vitamins and minerals, such as vitamin C, vitamin E, folic acid, potassium, magnesium and calcium.

Moroccan chicken

With its warm, fragrant, slightly sweet flavours, Moroccan food brings out the best in chicken. Use chicken breasts for this recipe, as they won't dry out. This recipe serves four.

ready in 25 minutes

4 chicken breasts (approximately 100g/3½oz each)

4 tablespoons olive oil

2 onions, chopped

2 garlic cloves, chopped or crushed

2x400g (13oz) cans chopped tomatoes

2 teaspoons fresh ginger, grated

2 cinnamon sticks

4 tablespoons orange juice

2 tablespoons lemon juice

300ml (½ pint) chicken stock *(see p.86)*

4 tablespoons fresh coriander, chopped

Cut each chicken breast diagonally into three strips. Heat 2 tablespoons of olive oil in a saucepan with a lid and gently brown the chicken breasts on both sides. Lift from the pan and put to one side.

Heat the rest of the olive oil in the same pan, add the onions and soften over a low heat. Add the garlic, tomatoes, ginger, cinnamon and orange and lemon juice and simmer together for about 5 minutes. Replace the chicken breasts, add the stock and combine well.

Bring to the boil and simmer very gently for about 10 minutes. Stir in the fresh coriander and serve on a bed of brown rice, quinoa or bulgar wheat with a salad of mixed leaves.

Baked sweet potato with feta Ⓥ

This is one of those meals that cooks itself and only needs minimal preparation before serving. Unlike ordinary potatoes, it doesn't matter if sweet potatoes are slightly al dente in the middle. Serves four.

4 sweet potatoes (150–200g/5–7oz each)

300g (11oz) feta cheese

2 plump spring onions

2 tablespoons olive oil

2 tablespoons orange juice

Freshly ground black pepper

2 rounded teaspoons caraway seeds (or fennel or cumin could be used instead)

A good handful fresh parsley, chopped

Preheat the oven to 180°C/350°F/gas mark 4.

Spear each potato with a metal kebab skewer to speed up the cooking time: the skewer will conduct the heat to the centre of the potato.

Cook the potatoes in the oven for about 40 minutes (depending on their size).

While the potatoes are cooking, chop or crumble the feta cheese into a small bowl. Finely chop the spring onions and toss them in with the feta cheese. Add the olive oil, orange juice and black pepper. Roast the seeds in small pan over a medium high heat to give a more intense, toasted flavour and stir them in with the feta. Leave to marinate while the potatoes are cooking.

When the sweet potatoes are cooked, remove from the skewer, cut them open and drizzle over a little olive oil. Scatter the feta mix on top, sprinkle with the chopped parsley and serve.

SERVING IDEAS

For lunch or dinner
This dish should make a filling lunch or dinner, so serve it with a simple crisp green salad. You can add some toasted seeds *(see p.127)* for extra protein or, if everyone is feeling very hungry, grill a few mini chicken breasts to serve with this dish.

Roast vegetable quinoa pilau

This recipe makes a tasty vegetarian main course, but you can halve the quantities and serve it as a side dish to accompany simply grilled meat or fish with the Roast pepper sauce on page 87. Serves four.

8 tablespoons olive oil

1 medium onion, finely chopped

2 garlic cloves, crushed or finely chopped

400g (14oz) quinoa, rinsed and drained

500ml (17fl oz) stock

20 baby plum tomatoes (approx 300g/10oz)

Freshly ground black pepper

12 baby courgettes (approx 350g/11½oz)

1 large yellow pepper

2 medium red onions, finely sliced

A few squeezes of lemon juice

1 teaspoon balsamic vinegar

½ teaspoon cinnamon powder

2 tablespoons fresh mint, chopped

Yellow peppers have a sweeter, more mellow flavour than green peppers, but still give cooked dishes plenty of colour and crunch.

Heat 2 tablespoons of olive oil in a large saucepan. Soften the onion over a low heat, add the garlic and stir. Add the drained quinoa, stir for a minute, then add the stock. Bring to the boil and simmer gently. It will take approx 20 minutes for the quinoa to cook, by which time all the stock should be absorbed.

Preheat the oven to 180°C/350°F/gas mark 4.

Cut the tomatoes in half, put them on a small baking tray, toss in 2 tablespoons of olive oil and season with a good grinding of black pepper. Roast in the oven for about 15 minutes until soft, with the juices running. When cooked, drizzle with the vinegar.

Slice the courgettes lengthways – about four slices to each small courgette – and slice the pepper into thin strips. Heat 2 tablespoons of olive oil in a griddle pan or frying pan, add the courgettes and pepper and cook over a medium heat for about 15 minutes, turning once, until brown on both sides.

Heat the final 2 tablespoons of olive oil in a frying pan, add the red onion and cook over a low heat for about 10 minutes, turning frequently, until it starts turning brown. Sprinkle with the cinnamon and cook for another couple of minutes.

Put the quinoa in a warmed bowl and toss with the tomatoes, courgettes and pepper, lemon juice, vinegar and a little olive oil. Top with the cinnamon, onions and the chopped mint. You can, if you wish, crumble some feta cheese on top too. Serve with a mixed leaf salad.

Spinach bake Ⓥ

This all-in-one dish is easy to make and tastes delicious. The combination of iron-rich spinach, nutritious eggs and mixed seeds makes this a balanced yet satisfying meal. Serves four.

SERVING IDEAS

For lunch If you have any flat breads in the freezer, serve them with the Spinach bake, or make some fresh flat breads *(see p.88)*.

For dinner Scatter some chopped fresh parsley on top of the dish for extra flavour.

2 or 3 large tomatoes (about 400g/13oz), sliced

1 medium onion, finely sliced

4 tablespoons olive oil

2 teaspoons balsamic vinegar

Freshly ground black pepper

2 garlic cloves, chopped

300g (10oz) spinach, washed and coarsely shredded

4 eggs

2 tablespoons live natural low-fat yoghurt

2 tablespoons ground The Food Doctor Chilli and Garlic Seed Mix, or grind 1 teaspoon chilli flakes, 1 crushed garlic clove and 2 tablespoons mixed pumpkin and sunflower seeds

Crumbled feta cheese as a garnish

Preheat the oven to 200°C/400°F/gas mark 6.

Put the tomatoes, onion, 2 tablespoons of olive oil and the vinegar in a roasting tin, season with freshly ground black pepper and roast until the onion is soft – about 45 minutes. Shake the tin occasionally to prevent burning. When cooked, roughly mash the vegetables together.

Heat a tablespoon of olive oil in a large saucepan, add the garlic and cook over a low heat for a minute. Add the spinach and cook until it has wilted.

Beat the eggs, yoghurt, ground seeds and black pepper together and make three flat omelettes *(see p.138)*.

Lightly oil a deep, round baking dish roughly the same size as the omelettes. Place one omelette in the bottom, cover with a third of the spinach and half the tomatoes and repeat. Top with the third omelette and the rest of the spinach. Scatter feta cheese on top, put in the oven for 10 minutes or under a grill to brown and serve.

Baked trout with fresh herbs

Trout is quite a delicate-tasting fish and only needs a few simple ingredients to bring out its flavour. Buy the freshest fish you can find on the day that you want to eat this dish. Serves four.

ready in 20 minutes

4 small trout, approx 150g (5oz) each without head

Juice 1 lemon

Freshly ground black pepper

4 small handfuls fresh herbs (use whatever is in season: dill, fennel, basil, parsley, chives, marjoram, mint or lemon balm)

75ml (5fl oz) dry white wine

SERVING IDEAS

For lunch or dinner
Serve each fish with a mixed leaf salad with added fresh herbs and hot, mashed chick-peas. Try serving some Yellow pepper sauce on the side *(see p.87)*.

Preheat the oven to 150°C/300°F/gas mark 2.

If you prefer, ask your fishmonger to gut the trout and remove its head. You could use two larger fish between four, but add an extra 5 minutes or so to the cooking time.

Rinse the fish to remove loose scales and wash the insides. Pat dry with kitchen paper and place in an oiled shallow ovenproof dish. Season the inside of the fish with lemon juice and black pepper and tuck a small handful of mixed fresh herbs into each cavity. Sprinkle the white wine over each fish, season with black pepper, cover the dish with foil and put in the oven to bake.

Small fish should only take 15 minutes to bake – the flesh should be just cooked but still nice and moist.

Stuffed gem squash

The easiest way to cut a squash in half is to use a very sharp knife and apply pressure with the heel of your free hand to back of the blade – or carefully hit the knife with a rolling pin. Serves four.

4 gem squashes

50g (2oz) bulgar wheat

250ml (8fl oz) light stock

2 tablespoons olive oil

1 medium onion, finely chopped

2 garlic cloves, finely chopped

250g (8oz) steak mince, as lean as possible

1 tablespoon smoked paprika

3–4 good sprigs fresh parsley, chopped

Freshly ground black pepper

300ml (½ pint) Rich tomato sauce *(see p.87)*

Cut each squash in half across its middle and scrape out the seeds. Put the squashes in a steamer to cook for 10 minutes until they are beginning to soften, but are not thoroughly cooked through.

Put the bulgar wheat in a bowl and pour in the boiling stock. Soak for 10 minutes, then squeeze the bulgar wheat through a fine sieve to remove excess moisture.

Preheat the oven to 170°/325°F/gas mark 3.

Heat the oil in a saucepan and soften the onion and garlic over a low heat. Turn up the heat a little, add the steak mince, break it up with a fork and stir until it is well browned. Stir in the paprika, then the bulgar wheat and parsley and season with freshly ground black pepper.

Put the squashes into a shallow baking dish and pack some of the stuffing into each squash, piling it up if necessary. Cover with foil and cook for half an hour, by which time the flesh of the squash should be soft.

Serve with the Rich tomato sauce and some Roasted root vegetables *(see p.68).*

Pot-roast chicken

It's worth cooking a large chicken, as you can use
the leftover cuts of meat for other recipes: Chicken
& avocado salad *(see p.42)*, Chinese chicken salad
(see p.41) and Chicken soup *(see p.93)*. Serves four.

1 chicken, about 2kg (4½lb)

1 medium onion

½ lemon

A few sprigs fresh thyme

Freshly ground black pepper

2 tablespoons olive oil

100ml (3½fl oz) white wine

A small handful fresh parsley, chopped

SERVING IDEAS

For lunch Serve with
some Roasted root
vegetables *(see p.68)*
and a small helping of
plain red or brown rice.

For dinner Lightly
steamed carrots and
courgettes are all you
need to serve with this
satisfying dish.

Preheat the oven to 180°C/350°F/gas mark 4.

Check that the cavity of the chicken is clear and then
stuff it with the onion and lemon. Tuck sprigs of fresh
thyme inside the chicken and under the wings and legs.
Drizzle the olive oil over the bird and season with black
pepper. Put the chicken in either a deep casserole with
a lid or a high dome-covered baking dish. Pour white
wine around the bird, cover and cook for 45 minutes.
Remove the lid and return to the oven for a further ten
minutes to brown the bird. Set the bird aside while you
tip the juices from the pan and the chicken cavity into
a small pan and skim off any fat.

Remove the skin, carve the bird and serve with a little
sauce poured over the meat.

Food
for friends

When you follow my principles, cooking for friends doesn't mean you have to compromise, as you will see from these impressive dishes.

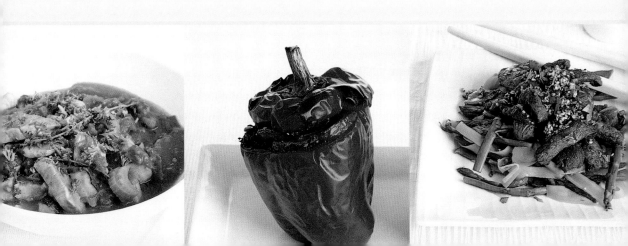

Moroccan stuffed peppers Ⓥ

Buy a mix of different coloured peppers to give
a more vibrant effect when you serve this dish.
It can be served as a vegetarian main course for
four people or as a starter for eight.

250g (9oz) red rice
3 tablespoons olive oil
400g (13oz) onions, finely chopped
400ml (¾pint) light stock
20g (1oz) currants
A small handful each mint, parsley and dill, finely chopped
25g (¾oz) pinenuts
8 peppers
1 large tomato (optional), sliced
50ml (2fl oz) water
1 tablespoon lemon juice
1 teaspoon olive oil

For the sauce:
3 tablespoons live natural low-fat yoghurt
3 tablespoons fat-reduced fromage frais
Juice ½ lemon
A couple of sprigs of fresh mint, finely chopped

Soak the red rice in cold water until needed.

Heat the oil in a large saucepan and soften the onion
over a low heat until it turns golden. Add the rice,
stock and currants and simmer for 30 minutes. Stir in
the chopped herbs and stir well.

Preheat the oven to 180°C/350°F/gas mark 4.

Add the pinenuts to the rice mix. Cut the stalk ends off
the peppers and scoop out the seeds and any pith. Fill
each pepper with the rice and top with a slice of tomato
(or you can put the cut end of pepper back on top).

Place the peppers upright in a baking dish positioned
fairly tightly together to support each other. Mix the
water, lemon juice and olive oil and pour it around the
base of the peppers. Cover with foil or a lid. Bake for
an hour until the peppers are soft, but not collapsing.

Mix the yoghurt, fromage frais, lemon juice and mint
together and serve separately in a small pot. Serve the
peppers with a watercress salad.

Chilli fish with stir-fried vegetables

Use any type of firm white fish for this recipe to match the fiery flavours of the chilli sauce. Sea bass, orange roughy or halibut are all good choices. Quantities for this recipe make enough for four.

4 white fish fillets, approx 75–100g (2½–3½oz) each

Freshly ground black pepper

850ml (1½ pints) fish stock

For the sauce:

4 tablespoons white wine

4 spring onions, finely chopped

4 garlic cloves, peeled whole

1 teaspoon chilli paste

1 teaspoon rice vinegar

For the stir-fry:

4 tablespoons olive oil

4 teaspoons caraway seeds

4 teaspoons brown mustard seeds

300g (10oz) sweet potato, grated

200g (7oz) bean sprouts

First, make the sauce: combine all the ingredients except the chilli paste and vinegar in a small pan, bring to the boil and simmer gently for about 15 minutes until the garlic is soft. Mash the garlic with a fork and stir in the chilli paste and vinegar.

Preheat the oven to 160°C/320°F/gas mark 3.

Place the fish fillets in a shallow dish and season with a good grinding of black pepper. Pour over the sauce, cover the dish with foil and bake for 10–15 minutes until the fish is just cooked.

Meanwhile, heat the oil in a wok, add the seeds and cook them until they pop. Throw in the sweet potato and bean sprouts and stir fry for 3–4 minutes until the vegetables are piping hot.

Pile the fish onto the stir-fried vegetables and serve with the chilli sauce spooned over the top.

Chilli paste is an easy way to use hot chillies in your cooking, but if you prefer to use fresh chillies, prepare them carefully. Wear washing up gloves to cut the chilli open lengthways and scoop out the fiery seeds. Then dice the chillies and add them to the pan with the other sauce ingredients.

Fish parcels with ribbon vegetables

This is a very quick and easy dish to serve for friends, and it looks impressive too. Keep the foil for each portion opened slightly when you serve it to prevent the fish cooking further. Serves four.

ready in **20** minutes

4 skinless white fish fillets, about 100g (3½oz) each

100g (3½oz) leeks

100g (3½oz) courgettes

200g (7oz) sweet potato

100g (3½oz) mangetout

100ml (3½fl oz) water

Juice 1 lemon

1 teaspoon fresh grated ginger

1 teaspoon soy sauce

4 tablespoons finely ground The Food Doctor Fennel and Caraway Seed Mix, or grind ½ teaspoon fennel seeds, ½ teaspoon caraway seeds and 2 tablespoons mixed pumpkin and sunflower seeds

Freshly ground black pepper

A large handful fresh coriander, finely chopped

1 lemon, quartered

Preheat the oven to 175°C/340°F/gas mark 4.

Cut the leeks finely lengthways into short strips, toss into boiling water for a couple of minutes to soften and then drain. Using a vegetable peeler, peel the courgettes and sweet potato into wide ribbons. Heat the water, half the lemon juice, ginger and soy sauce in a wok. Toss in the vegetables and stir fry for a minute or two.

Place the fish on a plate, drizzle each fillet with lemon juice and season with freshly ground black pepper. Coat each fillet in the ground seeds.

Cut four sheets of foil, large enough to wrap up each fish fillet, and lightly oil the surface of the foil. Lay a quarter of the vegetables on each sheet of foil and place a fillet on top. Carefully join the two long sides of foil and fold up the ends to make a loose parcel. Place the parcels on a baking sheet. Bake for 10–15 minutes, depending on the size of the fillet. The fish should be just cooked when you take it out of the oven.

Serve immediately in the parcel with the soy sauce from the wok and fresh coriander sprinkled on top. Add a wedge of fresh lemon at the side. This dish would go well with red rice or bulgar wheat.

Spicy fish stew

The better the fish stock, the tastier this stew is. Ask your fishmonger for offcuts and make a stock based on the chicken stock recipe on page 86, or buy a good-quality fish stock. Serves four.

400g (13oz) mixed fish fillets (tuna, salmon, sea trout, cod, coley, scallops or prawns)

Lemon juice to taste

Freshly ground black pepper

2 tablespoons olive oil

1 medium onion, finely chopped

1 stick celery, chopped

3 small courgettes (approx 200g/7oz), cut into thick chunks

1 garlic clove, finely chopped or crushed

1 bay leaf and 1 sprig thyme

½ teaspoon ground cumin seeds

1x200g (7oz) can chopped tomatoes

1 tablespoon tomato paste

2 teaspoons toasted sesame seed oil

75ml (3fl oz) white wine

150ml (¼ pint) fish stock

2 tablespoons fresh coriander, chopped

2 tablespoons The Food Doctor Chilli & Garlic Seed Mix, coarsely ground, or grind 1 teaspoon chilli flakes, 1 garlic clove and 2 tablespoons mixed pumpkin and sunflower seeds

Remove any skin from the fish fillets and cut them into large, bite-sized chunks. Put the pieces in a bowl, squeeze lemon juice over them, season with black pepper and leave to one side.

Heat the oil in a casserole and soften the onion and celery over a low heat. Add the courgettes and garlic and cook over a medium-high heat until the onion and celery start to take colour. Add the herbs and cumin seeds, tomatoes and paste and the sesame oil. Simmer for a couple of minutes and then pour in the white wine. Allow to bubble hard for a further minute or two. Pour in the stock, bring the stew to boiling point and simmer for about 15 minutes.

At this point, the stew can be cooled and kept in the fridge for up to 24 hours if you are preparing the dish in advance.

When you are ready to serve the stew, ensure that it is boiling before adding the fish pieces, then lower the heat and cook gently for 10–15 minutes. Just before serving, stir in the fresh coriander and ground seeds.

Serve in a bowl with a simple green salad and flat bread *(see p.88)* to mop up the juices.

Spiced duck breast

Indian five-spice powder is different to Chinese five-spice, and is available from any Asian store. However, you can easily make your own version if you prefer *(see p.150)*. This recipe serves four.

4 duck breasts

3 tablespoons ground Indian five-spice powder

1 teaspoon fresh ginger, grated

100ml (3½fl oz) live natural low-fat yoghurt

200g (7oz) bulgar wheat or quinoa, plus enough boiling stock to just cover the bulgar wheat

2 tablespoons olive oil

Rind 1 lemon, finely chopped

A small bunch fresh coriander, chopped

Juice and finely chopped rind ½ orange

3–4 sprigs fresh mint, chopped

Remove any skin and all the fat from each duck breast. Combine the five spice, ginger and yoghurt in a bowl and leave the duck breasts to marinate for at least half an hour, but preferably for a couple of hours.

Meanwhile, soak the bulgar wheat in boiling stock for 10 minutes, then drain. Stir in the olive oil, lemon rind and chopped coriander and keep warm. If using quinoa, simmer it gently in about 500ml (approx ¾ pint) of stock until the liquid has been absorbed and the quinoa is tender (add a little more stock if it boils away too fast). Add the olive oil, rind and coriander to the quinoa and keep the dish warm.

Warm a griddle over a medium-high heat and brush or spray it with olive oil. Wipe most of the marinade off the duck breasts and cook them on the griddle for 3–4 minutes on each side so that they are brown on the outside and still pink inside. Mix the orange and mint with the marinade, warm gently and serve separately.

A watercress side salad goes well with this dish.

Moroccan rabbit stew

You should be able to get rabbit from your butcher, or buy boned rabbit in most supermarkets, but if you can't, buy chicken thighs instead as their flesh is not dissimilar. This recipe serves four or more.

500g (1lb) tomatoes peeled and chopped, or 1x400g (13oz) can chopped tomatoes

1 rabbit, jointed, or 8 chicken thighs, skinned

4 tablespoons olive oil

3 medium onions, peeled and roughly chopped

1 garlic clove, chopped or crushed

1 whole cardamom pod, cracked

½ teaspoon allspice (or nutmeg if allspice is not available)

1 teaspoon cinnamon powder

40ml (2fl oz) red wine vinegar

50ml (2fl oz) unsweetened apple juice

Freshly ground black pepper

Approx 500ml (¾ pint) water

3 tablespoons fresh coriander or parsley, chopped

SERVING IDEAS
For lunch Serve with plain brown rice or bulgar wheat and a green salad.
For dinner Arrange a large mixed leaf salad or lightly steam a good quantity of vegetables to serve with the stew.

To peel the tomatoes, cover with boiling water and allow to stand for 5 minutes until the skins split. Drain and peel off the skins.

Heat the oil in a large casserole and brown the rabbit pieces, then lift them out and put them to one side. Tip the onions into the casserole and cook over a gentle heat until golden brown. Add the garlic and stir well.

Add the tomatoes, cardamom, allspice, cinnamon, vinegar, apple juice and rabbit pieces to the casserole, season with freshly ground black pepper and stir well. Pour in the water until it just covers the ingredients and bring to the boil. Turn the heat down low and simmer gently for an hour. Remove the lid, raise the heat slightly and simmer for half an hour to reduce the liquid.

Stir in the coriander or parsley and serve.

Calves' liver with coriander

You can also make this recipe using lambs' liver or venison liver, but if you use either of these alternatives, soak them in milk for half an hour before cooking to improve their flavour. Serves four.

ready in **10** minutes

400g (13oz) calves' liver
2 tablespoons chick-pea flour
2 tablespoons ground coriander
4 tablespoons olive oil
2 medium onions, chopped
100ml (3½fl oz) white wine
1 teaspoon soy sauce
200ml (7fl oz) very light hot stock
Juice and zest 2 large oranges
A large handful fresh coriander, chopped

Clean any stringy bits from the liver and cut into wide strips. Mix the flour and ground coriander in a shallow bowl and roll the pieces of liver in the flour.

Heat a tablespoon of olive oil and very quickly brown the liver – just a few seconds on each side. Lift the pieces from the pan and keep warm.

Heat the remainder of the oil and cook the onion until it starts to take colour. Meanwhile, stir the white wine and soy sauce into the hot stock. Then lift the onion from the pan and keep warm with the liver.

Pour the stock into the pan and bring it to the boil. Allow it to bubble, scraping up any residues in the pan. Add the orange juice and zest and return the liver and onion to the pan. Simmer very gently for 1 minute. Remove from heat, stir in the fresh coriander and serve with rosti *(see p.44)*.

Coriander is a strong, pungently flavoured fresh herb that can lift any dish. To store coriander, put it in a jar of water, cover the leaves with a plastic bag and keep in the fridge, changing the water every two days and picking out any wilted leaves.

Chinese five-spice lamb

Once you have marinated the lamb, this is a quick and impressive-looking dish to make for friends. Lean pork or beef would make a good alternative to lamb. Quantities listed are enough for four.

4 teaspoons Chinese five-spice paste *(see p.150)*

2 shallots, finely grated

2 tablespoons olive oil

Juice 1 lemon

2 teaspoons soy sauce

400g (13oz) lean lamb, cut into fairly large strips

Freshly ground black pepper

Juice 1 grapefruit

100ml (3½fl oz) water

200g (7oz) carrots

12 spears thin asparagus

4 small spring onions

300g (10oz) mangetout

2 tablespoons toasted sesame seeds *(see p.127)*

A small bunch fresh coriander, chopped

A drizzle of sesame oil

Put the spice, shallots, olive oil, lemon juice and soy in a bowl. Add the lamb, mix thoroughly, season with black pepper, and marinate for half an hour, or longer.

Clean the carrots and slice them into ribbons using a potato peeler (if they are very small, just cut them in half). Snap the tough ends off the asparagus and halve them. Cut the spring onions into thin strips. Bring a pan of water to the boil and simmer the asparagus for a couple of minutes to slightly soften them.

Heat the grapefruit juice and water in a wok over a high heat, add all the vegetables and boil quite fast until the juice has evaporated and the vegetables are just tender.

Cook the strips of lamb quickly on a hot griddle, or under a hot grill, turning frequently until well browned.

Serve the lamb on the vegetables, topped with toasted sesame seeds, the chopped coriander and a drizzle of sesame oil.

Stuffed pork fillet

The preparation time for this recipe takes about 20 minutes, so this task can be done ahead of time and the uncooked dish refrigerated for 24 hours if it's more convenient for you to do so. Serves four.

1x400–500g (13oz–1lb 2oz) pork fillet

Freshly ground black pepper

3 tablespoons lemon juice

2 tablespoons olive oil

1 medium onion, chopped

75g (3oz) mushrooms, chopped

1 dozen pitted black olives, coarsely chopped

1 tablespoon fresh parsley, chopped

1 tablespoon fresh sage, chopped

Zest 1 lemon

50ml (2fl oz) vegetable stock *(see p.86)*

(see p.86)

Cut five pieces of fine cooking string, each about 40cm (16in) long, and tie a slip knot with a tail at one end of each piece.

Lay the fillet on a board, slice halfway through the meat lengthways and fold the fillet out flat. Gently flatten the fillet by banging it with a rolling pin. Work the strings underneath the fillet so that they are evenly spaced with a piece near each end. Season with freshly ground black pepper and sprinkle with a tablespoon of lemon juice. Leave to one side while you make the stuffing.

Heat a tablespoon of oil in a pan and soften the onion over a low heat. Add the mushrooms, olives, herbs and lemon zest and season with a good grinding of pepper. Cook for 5 minutes, then spoon the mix down the centre of the fillet. Gently squeeze the sides together and hold in place with the string (pull one end through the slip knot and tighten). Start at the ends and work towards the middle, securing the knots as you go.

Preheat the oven to 180°C/350°F/gas mark 4.

Heat a tablespoon of oil in a frying pan over a high heat. Brown the meat all over and then place it in a shallow ovenproof dish. Pour the stock and lemon juice over the meat, cover with a lid or cooking foil and cook for half an hour before serving.

Osso bucco

This dish looks most impressive served on the bone, although the meat should fall away easily from the bone when you come to distribute it onto your guests' plates. Serves four.

1 slice of shin of veal, cut though the bone, weighing approx 500–600g (1lb–1lb 4oz) and about 8cm (3in) thick

2 tablespoons olive oil

400ml (¾ pint) Rich tomato sauce *(see p.87)*

150ml (¼ pint) dry white wine

For the gremolata:

2 tablespoons fresh parsley, chopped

1 teaspoon lemon zest, finely chopped

I garlic clove, chopped

Preheat the oven to 180°C/350°F/gas mark 4.

Heat the oil in a large saucepan over a high heat and brown the meat. Transfer to a casserole dish. Pour the wine into the pan and let it bubble for 30 seconds, then add the tomato sauce and bring to the boil. Pour this over the veal and transfer the dish to the oven to cook for about 45 minutes.

Mix the gremolata ingredients together just before serving and sprinkle a little over each portion.

> ### SERVING IDEAS
>
> **For lunch** Serve with steamed vegetables such as broccoli, flat bread *(see p.88)* and the sauce in a jug.
>
> **For dinner** Serve with the sauce in a jug and a large mixed leaf salad.

Lazy weekends

You don't have to be a slave to the kitchen all the time. These dishes are perfect for a lazy weekend and won't take much time to make.

Apple tonics

Make these delicious drinks to give you a boost at any time of day. Apples have beneficial effects on the digestive system and help to remove toxins, while ingredients such as lemon balm clear the mind and calm the nerves – perfect for a relaxing weekend. Serves two.

Love apple livener ⓥ

ready in **1** minute

200ml (7fl oz) tomato passata (cooked tomato concentrate)
200ml (7fl oz) unsweetened apple juice
1 teaspoon fresh ginger, grated
Pinch of cayenne pepper
Freshly squeezed lime juice to taste
2 slices lime

Mix the tomato passata and apple juice together. Add the ginger, cayenne and lime juice. Serve chilled with slices of lime.

Carrot & apple fizz ⓥ

ready in **1** minute

200ml (7fl oz) chilled carrot juice
200ml (7fl oz) unsweetened apple juice
400ml (¾ pint) sparkling water
Slices fresh lemon, lime and orange
A sprig lemon balm

Mix the chilled carrot juice and apple juice together and dilute with the sparkling water. Add the slices of lemon, lime and orange and the sprig of lemon balm and serve.

Apple zing ⓥ

ready in **10** minutes

200ml (7fl oz) boiling water
1 ginger tea bag
Juice 1 lemon
200ml (7fl oz) unsweetened apple juice
2 slices lemon

Pour the boiling water over the tea bag. Add the lemon juice and allow to cool. Mix in the apple juice and pour into glasses filled with ice cubes. Add a slice of lemon to each glass and serve.

Love apple livener

Carrot & apple fizz

Apple zing

Green tea with apple & mint Ⓥ

ready in 20 minutes

300ml (½ pint) boiling water

1 green tea tea bag

4 sprigs fresh mint

150ml (¼ pint) unsweetened apple juice

1 tablespoon lemon juice

2 slices apple

Pour the boiling water onto the tea bag and add two mint sprigs. Allow to cool, then mix in the apple juice and lemon juice. Chill, then serve with apple slices and the remaining sprigs of mint.

Green tea with apple & mint

Jasmine fruit compote with toasted seeds

You need to soak the dried fruit the night before you make this recipe, but it's so quick and easy to do that it won't feel like a chore. Vary the fresh fruits according to the season (such as raspberries, strawberries or blueberries), and use mint tea if you prefer. Serves two.

Jasmine fruit compote Ⓥ

ready in 5 minutes

150ml (5fl oz) green tea with jasmine

8 organic dried apricots, cut in half

6 dried prunes, cut in half

50ml (2fl oz) apple juice

½ crisp apple, cored and sliced

½ crisp pear, cored and sliced

Prepare by making the tea the night before. Allow to cool, add the dried fruit and steep overnight.

When you are ready to eat the compote, strain the tea off the fruit and stir the apple juice into it. Mix the fresh fruit with the soaked fruit in a bowl and pour over the juice. Top with a good dollop of the Fromage frais and yoghurt cream and a couple of tablespoons of toasted seeds *(see right)*.

You could also use the toasted Breakfast crunch, described on page 20, as an alternative topping.

Fromage frais & yoghurt cream Ⓥ

ready in 2 minutes

This is a delicious topping or base. Fromage frais has a better fat profile than crème fraiche.

2 tablespoons reduced-fat fromage frais

2 tablespoons live natural low-fat yoghurt

Beat the two ingredients together to make a soft, thick cream. You can also use this spread on flat bread *(see p.88)* with fruit on top.

Jasmine fruit compote

Toasted seeds

Toasted seeds ⓥ

ready in **5** minutes

1 tablespoon quinoa seeds
1 tablespoon sesame seeds
1 tablespoon pumpkin seeds
1 tablespoon sunflower seeds
1 tablespoon poppy seeds

Heat a heavy, dry pan until it's hot and toast each variety of seed separately. Cook the seeds for a couple of minutes, tossing them regularly as they pop and start to turn brown. Once cooked, combine the seeds in a bowl or keep them in an airtight container in the fridge for several weeks.

Haloumi brochettes with spicy salsa Ⓥ

This recipe makes a great barbecue dish or a quick evening meal. You can, if you wish, substitute the haloumi with fish, such as tuna, sword fish, monk fish or scallops. Quantities are enough for two.

ready in 15 minutes

4 thick slices of light haloumi cheese, approx 40g (1½oz) each

1 small courgette (approx 50g/2oz)

4 cherry tomatoes

8 small mushrooms (crimini mushrooms are small and firm and have a good flavour)

8 chunks red pepper

A drizzle olive oil

Cut the haloumi cheese into chunks. Soak four – or more, if you need them – wooden skewers in water, then thread the vegetables and cheese alternately onto the skewers: use something substantial such as a mushroom or courgette at either end, and position the tomato in the middle between the chunks of cheese.

Brush each brochette with a little olive oil and brown on a heated griddle, under a grill or on the barbecue. Turn frequently for even cooking and then serve.

Spicy salsa

35ml (1½fl oz) olive oil

½ tablespoon ground The Food Doctor Chilli Seed Mix, or grind ¼ teaspoon chilli flakes and ½ tablespoon sunflower seeds

½ spring onion, sliced

1 small chunk sweet red pepper

Juice ½ lime

2 teaspoons soy sauce

2 teaspoons orange juice

A sprig each fresh parsley, mint, coriander and basil

Put all the ingredients in a blender and blitz for a few seconds. The result should be coarse and chunky, not completely smooth. Pour the salsa into a bowl and serve with the brochettes.

SERVING IDEAS

For lunch Serve with the salsa and flat bread.

For dinner Arrange a large mixed salad to serve with the Haloumi brochettes and the salsa sauce.

Butter bean colcannon

Colcannon is usually made with mashed potato, but since mashed potato has a high GI rating, this recipe uses butter beans instead. The ham is optional if you want to make this a vegetarian dish. Serves two.

ready in **20** minutes

1x400g (13oz) can butter beans, drained and rinsed

Vegetable stock *(see p.86)* to cover the beans

2 teaspoons Dijon mustard

1 tablespoon reduced-fat fromage frais

2 good sprigs fresh parsley, chopped

2 tablespoons olive oil

100g (3½oz) onion, finely sliced

100g (3½oz) green cabbage, shredded

1 garlic clove, crushed

25ml (1fl oz) water

¼ teaspoon soy sauce

80g (3oz) lean ham, shredded

Put the beans in a saucepan and barely cover them with stock. Bring to boil and simmer for 5–10 minutes until the stock has reduced to about 25ml (1fl oz). Mash the beans with a potato masher, then mix in the mustard, fromage frais and parsley. Leave to one side in a bowl.

Heat a tablespoon of olive oil in a frying pan and soften the onion over a low heat. Add the cabbage and garlic and stir well. Add the water and soy sauce, turn the heat up and simmer, covered, for about 10 minutes until the cabbage is soft. Stir occasionally to prevent any ingredients sticking.

Tip the onion mix into the bowl of mashed beans and mix well. Then stir in the ham.

Heat the remaining oil in a non-stick frying pan and add the mash. Flatten it down to fill the pan and cook over a medium heat to brown the under side. Slip under a hot grill to brown the top before serving.

SERVING IDEAS

For lunch or dinner
This dish is filling enough to serve on its own, or if you are hungry you could cook one poached egg per person and serve them on top of the colcannon.

Cabbages are full of goodness, and are an ideal food to eat. If you find cabbage on its own tastes slightly bitter, a dish such as this is a perfect way to include this vegetable in your diet.

Easy toppings

This range of toppings can be spread on The Food Doctor High Bran and Seed Bagels, Mixed Cereal Puffed Crackers, flat breads or wraps, eaten with scrambled eggs, or even served together in small dishes like a mini tapas selection. All recipes serve two.

Roast tomatoes

ready in **15** minutes

8–10 cherry tomatoes
1 tablespoon olive oil
Freshly ground black pepper
Crumbled feta cheese as a garnish

Preheat the oven to 180°C/350°F/gas mark 4.

Put the tomatoes in a small roasting pan and toss in the black pepper and olive oil. Roast for 15 minutes or until soft and serve with the crumbled feta cheese.

Soft herring roes

ready in **5** minutes

4–6 herring roes
1 tablespoon olive oil
Freshly ground black pepper
Fresh lemon juice to taste

Rinse the roes and remove any discoloured bits. Heat the olive oil in a pan and gently sauté the roes until they are turning golden and curling into a ball. Season with black pepper and a little lemon juice and serve.

Sautéed mushrooms Ⓥ

ready in **10** minutes

200g (7oz) flat or exotic mushrooms
2 tablespoons olive oil
Freshly ground black pepper
Fresh lemon juice to taste
2 tablespoons fresh herbs, chopped

If the mushrooms are large, slice them finely; if small, leave whole or cut them in half. Heat the olive oil in a pan and sauté the mushrooms over a medium heat until they start to collapse and turn brown. Season with black pepper and lemon juice and add whatever fresh herbs you have in the fridge.

Roast baby tomatoes

Soft herring roes

Crab meat topping

Crab meat topping

ready in **10** minutes

25ml (1fl oz) reduced-fat fromage frais

25ml (1fl oz) live natural low-fat yoghurt

2 spring onions, finely chopped

½ teaspoon Dijon mustard

Zest and juice 1 lime

1 teaspoon fresh ginger, grated

A small handful fresh coriander, chopped

A few drops Tabasco sauce

Freshly ground black pepper

200g (7oz) crab meat

½ teaspoon Thai fish sauce

1 little gem lettuce, finely shredded

2 wedges fresh lemon

Put the fromage frais and yoghurt into a bowl and add the spring onions, mustard, lime juice and zest, ginger, coriander, Tabasco, black pepper and fish sauce. Mix well. Gently fold in the crab meat.

Put the shredded lettuce on top of two flat breads or wraps *(see p.25)* and spoon half the crab meat mix over each. Serve with a wedge of fresh lemon on each plate.

Lean ham

ready in **1** minute

Choose a lean ham baked on the bone in your local delicatessen or supermarket and have the slices cut very thinly. Arrange the slices of ham on a plate and serve.

Flat breads

Sautéed mushrooms

Lean ham

Smart salads for relaxed occasions

The great thing about these salads is that not only do they look impressive and taste delicious, they are all quick and easy to make using a can of chick-peas or lentils as a base ingredient. The quantities listed serve two, but can easily be increased to serve four or six people.

Warm chick-pea & seafood salad

ready in 10 minutes

2 tablespoons olive oil

1 garlic clove, crushed

1 teaspoon harissa paste

150g (5oz) can chick-peas

150g (5oz) cooked mixed seafood salad, available from most supermarkets

Juice 1 lemon

A good handful each fresh parsley and dill, coarsely chopped

Heat a tablespoon of olive oil in a pan over a low heat, add the garlic and allow it to take a little colour. Then add the harissa paste.

Drain and rinse the chick-peas and toss them in the hot oil for a couple of minutes. Allow them to get hot and begin to turn golden. Add the seafood salad and lemon juice and heat everything together gently.

Tip the contents of the pan into a salad bowl. Stir the fresh parsley and dill into the warm salad.

Serve with flat bread (see p.88) and a mixed leaf salad.

Artichoke, chick-pea & spinach salad ⓥ

ready in 5 minutes

150g (5oz) can chick-peas

100g (3½oz) artichokes marinated in oil (from a delicatessen or a jar)

½ red onion, finely chopped

A large handful baby spinach leaves

A small handful pitted black olives

For the dressing:

Juice ½ lemon

Freshly ground black pepper

3 tablespoons olive oil

Drain and rinse the chick-peas and tip them into a salad bowl. Drain and quarter the artichokes and combine them and the onion in the bowl with the chick-peas. Add the spinach leaves and olives.

To make the dressing, whisk the lemon juice, black pepper and olive oil together. Pour the dressing over the salad and toss the ingredients well to mix. Serve with some flat breads (see p.88).

Warm lentil & poached egg salad ⓥ

ready in 15 minutes

1 tablespoon olive oil

1 small onion, finely chopped

1 small carrot, finely chopped

1 small celery stick, finely chopped

1 red pepper, deseeded and roughly chopped

100g (3½oz) flat mushrooms, sliced

150g (5oz) can puy or brown lentils

2 eggs

50g (2oz) spinach

1 tablespoon balsamic vinegar

Freshly ground black pepper

Heat the oil in a saucepan and soften the onion, carrot and celery in the olive oil over a low heat. Cook for 5 minutes. Add the pepper and mushrooms and cook for a further 5 minutes.

Drain and rinse the lentils and add them to the pan. Stir everything together and heat up the lentils.

Heat up a large frying pan of water and poach the eggs (see p.23). While the eggs cook, add the spinach to to the lentil mix and cook until wilted.

Stir in the vinegar, spoon the mixture into bowls, season with black pepper, top with a poached egg and serve.

Mixed salad

Warm chick-pea
& seafood salad

Barbecue skewers

The beauty of these skewers is that even if you don't own a barbecue, you can use a medium-hot griddle or grill, pile the cooked skewers onto a plate and serve them outside. All recipes serve two; increase the quantities if you invite guests.

Skewers are **easy** to **prepare** and **quick** to **cook** so they are **idea** for a **lazy weekend** meal or snack

Flat bread

Turkey skewers with lime and basil salsa

Turkey skewers with lime & basil salsa

150–200g (5–7oz) boneless turkey

2 medium courgettes, cut into lengthways slices 7mm (¼in) thick

2 large red peppers, cut into 20 chunks

For the marinade:

2 teaspoons Chinese five-spice paste (see p.150)

Juice and zest 1 lime

2–3cm (¾in–1¼in) fresh ginger, grated

2 garlic cloves, crushed

1 tablespoon olive oil

2 teaspoons sesame oil

Freshly ground black pepper

For the salsa:

A small handful fresh basil, chopped

1 small green onion

½ yellow pepper

Freshly ground black pepper

1 garlic clove

2 tablespoons olive oil

Juice and zest ½ lime

Mix the marinade in a bowl, cut the turkey into 16 even-sized chunks and add to the marinade. Leave for at least half an hour in the fridge.

Blitz the salsa ingredients in a food processor for a few seconds.

To thread the skewers, partly wrap a piece of meat in a courgette slice, then alternately thread the peppers and wrapped meat onto four soaked wooden skewers. Cook on a griddle or barbecue for 15 minutes over a medium heat. Serve with the salsa, a green salad and flat bread.

Swordfish skewers with salsa

ready in **20** minutes

200g (7oz) swordfish steak, skinned

2 small courgettes, cut into thick slices

For the marinade:

Juice 1 lime

2 tablespoons olive oil

1 garlic clove, crushed or topped

2cm (¾in) fresh ginger, grated

Freshly grated black pepper

Soy sauce to taste

For the salsa:

50g (2oz) red onion, chopped

50g (2oz) cucumber, chopped

Cut the fish into 12 chunks. Mix the marinade in a bowl, add the fish and leave to marinate for at least 15 minutes.

Soak four wooden skewers in water, then alternately thread five slices of courgette and three pieces of fish on to each skewer (conserve the marinade). Cook on a barbecue or griddle over a medium heat to brown the courgettes and just cook the fish (overcooking the fish will leave it tough).

Tip the marinade into a food processor, add the onion and cucumber and blitz for a couple of seconds. Turn out into a small bowl and serve with the skewers and a little soy sauce.

Mediterranean chicken skewers

4 chicken thighs, each trimmed of fat and cut into three pieces

8 shallots or pickling onions

8 cherry tomatoes

100ml (3½fl oz) vegetable stock (see p.86)

For the marinade:

2 tablespoons olive oil

3 tablespoons lemon juice or white wine vinegar

1 teaspoon tomato paste

1 garlic clove, finely chopped

Freshly ground black pepper

A few sprigs fresh thyme, finely chopped (or ½ teaspoon dried thyme)

Combine the marinade ingredients in a bowl, add the chicken pieces and leave to marinate for at least 15 minutes, or longer if possible.

Put the shallots in a small saucepan, pour in the stock, bring to the boil and simmer for 5 minutes. Drain and set aside.

Soak four wooden skewers in water, then alternately thread two shallots, three chicken pieces and two baby tomatoes on each skewer, starting and ending with the shallots.

Grill on a barbecue or griddle over a medium heat until the chicken pieces are cooked through.

Serve with some Rich tomato sauce or Yellow pepper sauce (see p.87).

Weekend brunch rice dishes

A rice dish such as kedgeree is a classic brunch meal that is normally made with refined white rice. By substituting the white rice for brown or red rice, you can create "slow-burning" low-GI rice dishes that will supply you with steady energy levels for longer. All recipes serve two.

Orange rice with tofu

1 tablespoon olive oil

1 small onion, finely chopped

100g (3½oz) acorn squash, peeled and cut into 2cm (¾in) cubes

3 cardamom pods

Rind 1 orange (carefully peel the rind off the orange in large pieces so they can be lifted out before serving)

250ml (8fl oz) vegetable stock (see p.86)

100g (3½oz) red rice or brown Italian rice

150g (5oz) marinated tofu, cubed, or 3 hard-boiled eggs, roughly chopped

A small handful fresh mint or coriander, chopped

Freshly ground black pepper

Heat the oil in a medium-sized saucepan over a low heat and cook the onion, squash and cardamom pods until the onion has softened.

Add the orange rind and the stock to the pan and bring to a simmer. Add the rice, cover and simmer gently for 25 minutes. Remove the lid, stir in the tofu and cook for a further 5 minutes.

Add the mint or coriander, season with black pepper and add the chopped eggs if you are not using tofu. Remove the orange rind and cardamom pods and serve.

Coconut rice pilau Ⓥ

1 tablespoon olive oil

1 small onion, finely chopped

150g (5oz) brown Italian rice (short grain)

300ml (½ pint) vegetable stock (see p.86)

60g (2oz) creamed coconut

1 teaspoon ground turmeric

Freshly ground black pepper

A small bunch parsley, finely chopped

Juice ½ lemon

3 hard-boiled eggs

Soften the onion in the olive oil over a low heat. Add the rice and stir for a few seconds. Pour in the hot stock and bring to a simmer. Add the coconut and stir until dissolved. Simmer for 20–25 minutes until the rice is cooked.

Stir in the turmeric, black pepper to taste, parsley and lemon juice. The liquid should be almost absorbed but with some creamy juice still left. If the rice has absorbed the liquid too quickly, add another 50ml (2fl oz) hot stock.

Divide between two plates with the hard-boiled eggs cut into quarters and arranged around the rice. Garnish with some more chopped fresh parsley and serve.

Red rice kedgeree

1 flat teaspoon cumin seeds

450ml (¾ pint) boiling water

150g (5oz) red rice

200g (7oz) smoked haddock, undyed

1 tablespoon olive oil

A little grated nutmeg

½ teaspoon ground turmeric

1 tablespoon lemon juice

Freshly ground black pepper

2 tablespoons fresh parsley, chopped

2 tablespoons live natural low-fat yoghurt

2 poached eggs (see p.25)

For the poaching flavouring:
1 lemon slice

1 sprig fresh parsley

1 bay leaf

4 black peppercorns

Dry roast the cumin seeds in a large hot pan for a few seconds until they pop. Pour the boiling water into the pan, add the rice and simmer for 25 minutes.

Put the poaching flavourings and fish in a saucepan. Add cold water until the fish is just covered. Bring to the boil over a medium heat. Turn off the heat and leave for 10 minutes. Drain. Flake the fish, remove any skin or bones and put in a bowl.

Combine the olive oil, nutmeg, turmeric, lemon juice and black pepper. Drain the rice and combine with the fish and parsley in an ovenproof dish. Serve with the two poached eggs and yoghurt poured over the top.

Red rice kedgeree

Deluxe omelette

This is a versatile recipe that can easily be adapted, so it's perfect if you need to use up any leftovers in the fridge. It's also delicious eaten cold if you want to save some to eat later as a snack. Serves two.

ready in 25 minutes

2 tablespoons white wine

2 tablespoons water

½ teaspoon Thai fish sauce

A couple sprigs fresh tarragon

100g (3½oz) salmon fillet

3 tablespoons pinenuts

100g (3½oz) fresh asparagus (weight after snapping off the tough end of the stalk)

4 tablespoons reduced-fat fromage frais

Juice and rind ½ lime

4 eggs

4 tablespoons live natural low-fat yoghurt

Freshly ground black pepper

A small handful tarragon sprigs, chopped

Pour the wine, water and fish sauce into a pan and add the sprigs of tarragon. Bring to the boil and put the salmon in, skin side down. Lower the heat to a gentle simmer and cook for 10–15 minutes until the salmon is just cooked through. Lift the fish from the pan, remove the skin and coarsely flake the fish.

Toast the pinenuts in a dry pan over a medium heat, tossing frequently, until they are brown on all sides.

Steam the asparagus until just cooked – about 5–6 minutes. Cut each asparagus stalk into 3 pieces.

Mix the fromage frais and lime juice and rind together in a bowl. Gently fold in the asparagus and fish.

To make the omelettes, beat the eggs, yoghurt, black pepper and tarragon together in a bowl and use half the mixture to make the first omelette.

Heat a little oil in a frying pan, pour in the egg mix and cook over a medium heat. When the omelette is set underneath but still soft on top, spread half the filling over one side of the omelette, sprinkle half the nuts on top and carefully fold the plain half of the omelette over the filling. Leave to cook for a few seconds to set the omelette a little more. Keep it warm in the oven while you make the second omelette, then serve.

SERVING IDEAS

For lunch Serve with a mixed leaf salad and flat bread (see p.88).

For dinner Add some herbs for extra flavour and serve with a large mixed leaf salad.

Herby scrambled eggs

Although this is such a simple recipe, it's important that you don't overcook the eggs. Aim for a soft, creamy consistency; if the eggs become watery or rubbery, they've been cooked too long. Serves two.

`ready in` **5** `minutes`

4 small eggs

A drizzle of olive oil

A pinch of ground turmeric

Freshly ground black pepper

A small handful fresh herbs (dill, coriander, sage, and marjoram), chopped

Break the eggs into a bowl, season with black pepper and a pinch of turmeric and whisk together.

Heat a little olive oil (or, for a treat, use unsalted butter) in a heavy, non-stick pan over a medium heat. Pour in the egg mixture and move the eggs slowly around the pan. Cook until the eggs set into soft flakes. Once cooked, stir in plenty of chopped fresh herbs and serve immediately with wholemeal toast or rye bread.

Smoked salmon pasta

This is a quick and tasty recipe that makes a perfect weekend meal at any time of day. The hot pasta and fresh-tasting fromage frais help to bring out the flavour of the smoked salmon. Serves two.

ready in **15** minutes

100g (3½oz) corn pasta shells

A drizzle of olive oil

A drizzle of lemon juice

50ml (2fl oz) reduced-fat fromage frais

50ml (2fl oz) live natural low-fat yoghurt

1 tablespoon olive oil

100g (3½oz) smoked salmon

Freshly ground black pepper

A small bunch fresh dill, chopped

Cook the pasta according to the instructions on the packet. Once cooked, strain and toss in a little olive oil and lemon juice.

Combine the fromage frais and yoghurt with the tablespoon of olive oil.

Cut the smoked salmon into strips. Combine the salmon with the pasta and the yoghurt mix. Season with black pepper and lemon juice to taste. Stir in the chopped dill and serve with a side salad of fresh chicory mixed with sprigs of fresh parsley.

Smoked salmon, eggs & spinach

Salmon is high in omega-3 essential fats, so it's a good choice of protein. Whether you buy slices of smoked salmon or offcuts, check that the salmon is fresh and moist, but not shiny. Serves two.

ready in 10 minutes

100g (3½oz) spinach, cleaned

1 tablespoon reduced-fat fromage frais

1 tablespoon live natural low-fat yoghurt

2 eggs

80g (3oz) smoked salmon, cut into wide strips

A drizzle of fresh lemon juice

Freshly ground black pepper

A pinch of paprika

If the spinach leaves are large, shred them coarsely. Steam them for about 5 minutes until the leaves are limp. Drain well and keep warm.

Combine the yoghurt and fromage frais in a small bowl and then poach the eggs *(see p.25)*.

Combine the smoked salmon and spinach leaves, drizzle with lemon juice and season with black pepper and divide onto two plates. Top each serving with a poached egg and spoon over the yoghurt mixture. Sprinkle with paprika and serve with flat bread on the side or beneath the salmon and spinach leaves.

Smoked salmon is made by curing fresh salmon fillets in salt to draw out the moisture and then smoking them in a kiln. This gives smoked salmon its distinct flavour, and helps retain its essential nutrients.

Occasional desserts

Eating sweet food perpetuates the feeling of wanting more, so don't have these delicious desserts too often.

Poached pears Ⓥ

It doesn't matter too much whether the pears you use for this recipe are slightly hard: poaching the fruit will soften their flesh and bring out more of their flavour. Serves two.

2 pears

250ml (8fl oz) jasmine tea

1 tablespoon unsweetened apple juice

½ small stick cinnamon

1 clove

2 mint leaves

½ teaspoon arrowroot powder

2 tablespoons live natural low-fat yoghurt or reduced-fat fromage frais

Peel the pears, removing the black part of the core that shows and leaving the stalk intact. Put the pears in a saucepan large enough to hold them both and add the jasmine tea, apple juice, spices and mint leaves. Simmer for 10–15 minutes, by which time the pears should be soft but still holding their shape.

Lift the pears from the pan and put them into a serving dish. Rapidly boil the fluid in the pan, reducing it to about 200ml (7fl oz).

Mix the arrowroot in a small cup with 2 tablespoons of cold water. Add a little of the tea mix from the pan and stir well. Pour this mix back into the pan and stir well over a low heat. Simmer for a couple of minutes, stirring all the time until the mixture has thickened to a syrupy consistency. Pour the sauce over the pears and chill in the fridge.

Serve with a tablespoon of natural yoghurt or fromage frais and some sauce poured over each pear.

Buy organic pears when they are in season if you want to have the best flavour and texture.

Baked apples

Hot, aromatic baked apples straight from the oven
are a delicious occasional treat, but take care that
they don't explode as you cut through the skin.
They also taste good cold. Serves two.

2 good-sized crisp eating apples

40g (2oz) mixed raw unsalted nuts, coarsely ground

4 dried apricots, finely chopped

¼ teaspoon ground cinnamon or mixed spice

2 tablespoons reduced-fat fromage frais

Preheat the oven to 170°C/325°F/gas mark 3.

Use an apple corer or a thin, sharp knife to remove the
core from each apple.

Mix the nuts, apricots and spice together and stuff the
mixture into the hole at the centre of each apple,
making sure it is packed in all the way through the
hole. Put the stuffed apples in a roasting dish, cover
with cooking foil and bake for 45 minutes to an hour,
depending on the size of the apples. When the flesh is
soft, serve hot with a tablespoon of fromage frais beside
each baked apple.

Summer berry compote Ⓥ

Choose raspberries, blueberries, blackberries, strawberries, blackcurrants or redcurrants as they come into season. Blackcurrants have a very strong flavour, so don't use too many. Serves two.

300ml (½ pint) mint tea

600g (1lb 4oz) mixed red berries

100ml (3½ fl oz) unsweetened apple juice

2 tablespoons reduced-fat fromage frais

Make the mint tea using 2 teabags and leave to infuse for 10 minutes. Then put the tea into a saucepan with the apple juice and boil the liquid until it reduces down to about 100ml (3½fl oz).

Put the mixed berries in a pan over a very low heat, pour in the mint tea and bring to the boil. Take off the heat, stir and chill in the fridge.

Serve with a tablespoon of fromage frais on top of each portion of berries.

Summer berries are packed with antioxidants. Store them in the fridge and eat them soon after purchasing for maximum freshness and nutritional benefit.

Chocolate pots

It's worth buying the best-quality dark chocolate you can find with at least 70-per cent minimum cocoa solids – it will make a real difference to the flavour. Serves two.

40g (1½oz) plain, very dark chocolate

2 tablespoons hot water

4 tablespoons reduced-fat fromage frais

A few toasted nuts, coarsely ground

Break the chocolate into a bowl and put it over a saucepan of boiling water (making a *bain marie*). Simmer the water until the chocolate has melted. Stir in the hot water and mix well to make a thick, shiny paste. Cool, then stir in the fromage frais.

Divide the chocolate mix between two small espresso coffee cups and put in the fridge to chill.

Toast the nuts by cooking them in a hot, heavy dry pan for a couple of minutes and then grinding them in a pestle and mortar.

When the chocolate pots are chilled, top each portion with a few toasted nuts and serve.

Apricot & oat fingers

Oats are low in gluten and high in fibre, so they are a beneficial food to include in your diet. They also have a low GI rating, releasing energy slowly, so you should find this recipe filling. Serves two.

7 dried apricots, plus enough mint tea to just cover them
40g (2oz) rolled oats
50ml (2fl oz) mint tea (reserved)
30g (1oz) coarsely ground mixed nuts

For the dip:
1 passion fruit
2 tablespoons reduced-fat fromage frais

Soak the apricots in enough boiling mint tea to cover them generously and leave for 3 hours until soft, or simmer very gently for about half an hour.

Preheat the oven to 180°C/350°F/gas mark 4.

Lift the apricots from the tea and purée them in a food processor. Put the oats into a saucepan, add the puréed apricots and pour in the reserved mint tea and the nuts. Mix well and cook over a low heat for a few minutes.

Oil a small baking sheet and press the mixture onto it – it shouldn't be too thick – and then bake in the oven

for 20 minutes. If the top is not as brown as you would like when you take the oat mix out of the oven, brush the top with a little oil and slip under a hot grill for a couple of minutes until it takes on a deep golden colour.

While the apricot and oat fingers are cooking, make the dip by cutting the passion fruit in half and scooping the seeds and yellow flesh into a bowl (be careful to leave all the pith behind). Mix with the fromage frais.

Cut the apricot and oat bake into slim fingers and serve warm with the passion fruit dip.

Mango & cardamom frozen yoghurt Ⓥ

If you like frozen yoghurt with a lighter texture, include the egg white in this recipe; if you prefer a stronger flavour, leave it out. This makes enough for four, so leave two portions in the freezer.

1 large, ripe mango

100ml (3½oz) live natural low-fat yoghurt

100ml (3½oz) reduced-fat fromage frais

2 cardamom pods

1 large egg (optional)

2 teaspoons lemon juice

Zest ½ orange, finely grated

2 passion fruit

Peel the mango and slice the flesh off the stone. Put the flesh in a blender and blitz for a few seconds until it's puréed. Tip the purée into a bowl and stir in the yoghurt and fromage frais.

Scrape the black seeds from the cardamom pods into a pestle and mortar and grind them to a powder. Tip into the mango mix with the orange zest and stir well.

If using the egg, separate the yolk from the white and whisk the white until stiff. Fold into the mango mix.

Put the mango mix into two freezer containers and freeze. If you don't have an ice-cream maker, stir the semi-frozen mix a couple of times before it freezes in order to prevent hard crystals forming.

To serve, leave the frozen yoghurt at room temperature for about 20 minutes to soften a little before scooping it into bowls. Top each serving with the seeds and yellow flesh squeezed from half a passion fruit and a little orange zest sprinkled over the top.

Useful Ingredients

Chilli paste

Hot chillies, vinegar, garlic, shallots and tamarind are some of the ingredients of most chilli pastes. They give chilli paste a sweet, hot and tangy flavour, which can be used with stir-fries or soup and as a dipping sauce or a salad dressing.

Chinese five-spice powder

The five flavours in this seasoning, from which it gets its name, are salty, sour, bitter, pungent and sweet. This powder is quite pungent, so use sparingly.

6 star anise

2 teaspoons ground cassia or cinnamon

2 teaspoons cloves

1 tablespoon ground fennel seeds

1 tablespoon Szechuan pepper

Grind all the ingredients in a food processor or blender until very fine. Sieve and store in an airtight container.

Feta cheese

This salty, fresh-tasting white cheese is traditionally made with sheep's or goats' milk – although some large commercial producers often make it with cows' milk. Feta cheese is usually sold in large slices (feta means "slice"), which can range from soft to semi-hard in texture, and are packed in brine. It has a lower fat profile than other hard cheeses, which makes it a useful ingredient to use for The Food Doctor Everyday Diet. Its versatility means that it is equally delicious crumbled over salads or used in cooked dishes.

Five-spice paste

Use either the Chinese or Indian five-spice powder recipes listed on these pages if five-spice powder is unavailable in your local shops, or substitute a small pinch of cinnamon and clove to your cooking.

2 tablespoons five-spice powder

2 garlic cloves, crushed

1 tablespoon soy sauce

Blend all the ingredients into a paste and store in a screw-top jar in the fridge for up to a week.

Fromage frais

A fresh, white curd cheese made from cows' milk, fromage frais has a creamy consistency, similar to cream cheese, and a mild, fresh taste. It contains very little fat and is low in cholesterol. It has a better fat profile than crème fraiche (which is soured, thickened cream) and is ideal used in cooking. It also tastes good uncooked as a topping for both savoury and sweet dishes. Reduced-fat fromage frais is virtually fat-free.

Haloumi cheese

This semi-hard white cheese, which traditionally comes from Cyprus, is made from sheep's milk and has a clean, mild taste. It is often made with dried mint. Like feta cheese, haloumi – and especially haloumi light cheese – has a lower fat content than other hard cheeses. It is best served grilled or baked and eaten immediately.

Herbes de Provence

The herbs used in this classic mix can vary considerably. Choose herbs of your choice in the quantities listed below, or follow this recipe:

3 tablespoons dried thyme

2 tablespoons dried marjoram

1 teaspoon dried rosemary

1 tablespoon dried savory

1 teaspoon dried lavender flowers

Crumble or grind the herbs and store in an airtight jar for 2–3 months.

Horseradish sauce

This sauce is commonly served with roast beef, fish or poultry, or with vegetables such as courgettes or beetroot. Rather than opt for bought horseradish sauce, which may contain preservatives, it's just as easy to make your own version. This recipe makes enough for four servings:

125g (4oz) live natural low-fat yoghurt

2 tablespoons fresh horseradish, grated

2 teaspoons fresh dill, chopped

Freshly ground black pepper

Mix all the ingredients together in a bowl. Store, covered, in the fridge until needed.

If you wish to serve the horseradish sauce warm, heat it gently over a saucepan of simmering water, but ensure that it does not boil because this will make the sauce curdle.

Indian five-spice powder

To make your own Indian five-spice powder, use the following ingredients:

2 teaspoons cumin seeds

2 teaspoons fennel seeds

1 teaspoon black mustard seeds

1 teaspoon black onion seeds

½ teaspoon fenugreek

Grind all the ingredients together in a blender or food processor until they turn into a fine powder. Sieve the powder and store in an airtight container.

Miso paste

Made from fermented soya beans, Japanese miso paste is usually mixed with water to make a savoury soup that is traditionally served as a first course or a quick snack. Miso paste comes in different colours, from light straw to dark brown. It has a savoury flavour and, generally, the lighter the miso, the milder it is. Try brushing a thin layer of the paste onto chicken or fish fillets before baking or grilling them. Miso is also available as a soup powder, which is a good substitute if the paste is unavailable. The powder can be sprinkled onto stir-fries for extra flavour, or mixed with live natural low-fat yoghurt to make a dip. Miso paste and powder may be available in the oriental foods section of a supermarket, or from an Asian store.

Rice wine

Another oriental product, rice wine is a sweet wine made from fermenting steamed glutinous rice, which has quite a low alcohol content. The better known rice wines, saki and mirin, come from Japan.

Soy sauce

Soy sauce is extracted from boiled soya beans that have been fermented with barley or wheat, then salted and fermented again. Choose a light sauce if possible for use in cooking and a dark sauce as a condiment to be sprinkled sparingly (it is very salty) over finished dishes.

Tabasco sauce

This hot, spicy sauce is made from red peppers, vinegar and salt. The peppers are aged for up to three years in salt and then mixed with the vinegar to give a pungent, fiery taste.

Tamarind paste

Tamarind pods look like long dates and the pulp inside, which has a distinctive sour, fruity flavour, is used as a souring agent.

Thai fish sauce

Often labelled simply "fish sauce", this ingredient is sold in the oriental foods section in the supermarket. Thai fish sauce is a very salty, thin, brown liquid used in Malay and Thai cooking, when it is called *nam pla*.

The sauce is made by fermenting fish or shrimps with salt. If it is not available, anchovy essence makes an acceptable substitute.

Thai fry paste

Most concentrated Asian pastes like this one contain ingredients such as coriander, ginger, garlic, lemon grass, chilli, fish sauce and lime juice, which all give a hot, tangy flavour to your cooking. Use in moderation.

The Food Doctor seed mixes

These mixes of sunflower, sesame, pumpkin, hemp seeds and linseeds are roasted in a light soya-like sauce called *koji*, and will keep well in their airtight containers. All five seed mixes are high in protein, low in carbohydrates, gluten-free and rich in omega-6 essential fatty acids. They can be added to soups, salads and stir-fries for extra flavour and crunch, ground into a powder to be used in cooking or eaten as a snack with a piece of fruit.

Tofu

This ingredient of Chinese and Japanese cooking is made from puréed soy beans. Bean curd is soft and white, with a cheese-like texture that ranges from firm to silken. It is high in protein and very low in fat.

Firm tofu is used largely as a salad ingredient, added in bite-sized cubes. Silken tofu is the best tofu for cooking. It is used largely for blending into other ingredients to make a range of sauces.

Tofu is also available marinated or smoked. These variations are best used in salads or stir-fries.

Beneficial foods

The recipes in this book use a range of ingredients, which are all included because of their nutritional benefits to your health. If there are some foods you have never tried before or that you are not sure you like, check the lists here to see why these top beneficial foods are worth including in your diet.

Apples
An ideal food. Apples are high in calcium, magnesium, phosphorus, vitamin C and beta-carotene. They also help to relieve constipation, remove toxins and reactivate beneficial gut bacteria.

Asparagus
A good source of folate and vitamin E, asparagus can help to maintain healthy gut bacteria if eaten regularly. Steaming, not boiling, helps preserve its fibre content.

Avocado
An ideal food. Avocado is high in essential fats and vitamin E and is easily digested.

Beans (broad, green, runner)
As with all green vegetables, fresh beans are a good source of minerals such as magnesium and calcium.

Beetroot
Contains calcium, potassium, folic acid and vitamin C. Beetroot is also an excellent intestinal cleanser.

Broccoli
An ideal food. Broccoli is full of fibre, especially if eaten raw. It's high in vitamins and minerals such as vitamin C, beta-carotene and folic acid, and is high in antioxidants.

Cabbage
An ideal food. Cabbage is high in nutrients and fibre and stimulates the immune system. Raw cabbage also detoxifies the stomach and improves digestion.

Celeriac
A member of the celery family, celeriac is an excellent source of fibre. It contains the nutrients calcium, magnesium, potassium and vitamin C, and is considered beneficial to the nervous and lymphatic systems.

Chick-peas
An excellent source of vegetable protein, chick-peas are also high in fibre, iron and folate. They can help to lower cholesterol and are a good digestive cleanser.

Chicken
An ideal source of lean protein. Buy free-range or organic chicken to ensure the meat is free of hormones and chemicals. (Feathered game such as pheasant and duck are also good energy-producing foods.)

Eggs
High in protein and low in cholesterol. Eggs also contain vitamins A and D, folate and calcium. An energy food.

Fish
All fish, and especially oily varieties such as herring, mackerel, salmon, sardines and tuna, are rich sources of beneficial essential oils, which are good for hormonal health, skin, bones, teeth and the immune system.

Garlic
Garlic cloves contain calcium, phosphorus, potassium and vitamin C, help to lower cholesterol and are well known to be a natural antibiotic.

Ginger
Contains calcium, magnesium, phosphorus and potassium. Ginger is also known to prevent nausea, improve circulation and is excellent for convalescence.

Lemons
High in vitamin C and potassium. Lemons are a potent natural antiseptic so they are an excellent natural remedy for colds, coughs and sore throats.

Lentils and other pulses
Pulses such as lentils, haricot, flageolet, mung and butter beans are an ideal source of vegetable protein. They are also a good source of minerals, such as zinc and folic acid, which are needed by nearly every organ in the body.

Leeks
High in antioxidants, leeks contain vitamins A and K, potassium, calcium and folic acid. Steaming helps preserve their fibre content.

Mushrooms
All types stimulate the immune system, thin the blood and lower cholesterol. Mushrooms are high in nutrients, including vitamins B3 and B5, iron and zinc. Shiitake mushrooms are known to have key health benefits.

Nuts
Raw unsalted nuts such as walnuts, cashew nuts, almonds, pinenuts and Brazil nuts are all high in protein, essential fats and vitamins and minerals.

Oats
The high fibre content of oats stimulates digestive function. Excellent for bones and connective tissue. Oats are also high in minerals and vitamin B5.

Onions
Benefits include antibiotic, antiseptic and detoxifying properties. Onions also contain minerals such as calcium, magnesium, folic acid and phosphorus.

Olive oil
High in Omega-6 essential fats.

Oranges
Known for their vitamin C content, oranges also contain calcium, potassium, beta-carotene and folic acid. The fruit has stimulating and cleansing effects.

Pears
High in fibre and iodine, which is beneficial for thyroid function. Pears also contain important minerals.

Peas
Freezing does not affect the vitamin and mineral content of peas. They are a good source of vegetable protein, and help to aid liver function.

Peppers
All peppers, whatever their colour or size, contain good levels of potassium, beta-carotene, folic acid and vitamins B and C. They also improve the circulatory system.

Quinoa
An ideal vegetable protein. Quinoa is easy to digest, is gluten-free and contains more calcium than milk. It's high in nutrients such as iron, potassium and vitamin B3.

Rice (brown and red)
Known as an energy food, brown or red rice is high in fibre, is calming to the nervous system and contains necessary B vitamins and minerals.

Seeds
Linseeds, pumpkin, sunflower, and sesame seeds are all high in protein, essential fats and minerals and vitamins. Sunflower seeds and linseeds are considered perfect foods.

Squash
High in antioxidants, squashes also contain good levels of calcium, magnesium, phosphorus, magnesium, potassium, beta-carotene and vitamin C.

Spinach
An ideal food. Spinach boosts the immune system and is high in nutrients such as iron, B vitamins and folic acid, especially if eaten raw.

Sweet potato
Easily digestible and highly nutritious, sweet potatoes are excellent for inflammation of the digestive tract, ulcers and poor circulation. They are also detoxifying and contain nutrients such as vitamins C and E and folic acid.

Tofu
An ideal source of vegetable protein. Tofu balances hormones, lowers cholesterol and contains necessary nutrients such as vitamins A and K, calcium and iron.

Tomatoes
High in antioxidants, tomatoes also contain good levels of calcium, magnesium, beta-carotene and vitamin C.

Yoghurt (natural)
Live yoghurt contains beneficial bacteria that soothe the intestinal tract and maintain good levels of gut bacteria.

Watercress
One of the best foods for purifying the blood. Contains high levels of iodine and other beneficial nutrients.

Essential shopping lists

The following foods are all used in various recipes in this book. Use these lists as a reminder to yourself to stock up with the ingredients – or use them as checklists when you shop – so that when the time comes you can easily prepare many of the dishes featured.

Grains & wheat
- ☐ Barley flakes
- ☐ Brown basmati rice
- ☐ Brown Italian rice
- ☐ Buckwheat flour
- ☐ Buckwheat noodles
- ☐ Bulgar wheat
- ☐ Chick-pea flour
- ☐ Corn pasta shells
- ☐ Gram flour
- ☐ Maize flour
- ☐ Oat flakes
- ☐ Oatcakes
- ☐ Quinoa
- ☐ Quinoa flakes
- ☐ Red rice
- ☐ Rye/wholemeal bread
- ☐ The Food Doctor High Bran and Seed Bagels
- ☐ Wholemeal bread

Pulses
- ☐ Butter beans, canned
- ☐ Cannellini beans, canned
- ☐ Chick-peas, canned
- ☐ Flageolet beans, canned
- ☐ Lentils, green, red and Puy, dried or canned
- ☐ Mung beans, dried
- ☐ Spilt yellow peas, dried

Nuts & seeds
- ☐ Cashew nuts
- ☐ Hazelnuts
- ☐ Hemp seeds

- ☐ Linseeds
- ☐ Pinenuts
- ☐ Poppy seeds
- ☐ Pumpkin seeds
- ☐ Quinoa seeds
- ☐ Sesame seeds
- ☐ Sunflower seeds
- ☐ The Food Doctor Chilli and Garlic Seed mix
- ☐ The Food Doctor Fennel and Caraway Seed Mix
- ☐ The Food Doctor Original Seed Mix
- ☐ The Food Doctor Rosemary and Onion Seed Mix
- ☐ The Food Doctor Sage and Thyme Seed Mix

Herbs
- ☐ Basil
- ☐ Bay leaves
- ☐ Chives
- ☐ Coriander
- ☐ Dill
- ☐ Herbes de Provence (dried)
- ☐ Lemongrass
- ☐ Marjoram
- ☐ Mint
- ☐ Mixed herbs, dried
- ☐ Oregano, dried
- ☐ Parsley
- ☐ Rosemary
- ☐ Sage
- ☐ Tarragon
- ☐ Thyme (fresh and dried)

Spices
- ☐ Allspice
- ☐ Black pepper
- ☐ Caraway seeds
- ☐ Cardamom pods
- ☐ Chilli paste
- ☐ Chilli powder
- ☐ Cinnamon, ground
- ☐ Cinnamon, sticks
- ☐ Cloves
- ☐ Coriander seeds
- ☐ Cumin powder
- ☐ Cumin seeds
- ☐ Chinese five-spice paste
- ☐ Cloves
- ☐ Fennel seeds
- ☐ Indian five-spice paste
- ☐ Ginger, fresh
- ☐ Ginger powder
- ☐ Mustard seeds, black
- ☐ Nutmeg
- ☐ Nutmeg powder
- ☐ Paprika, smoked or unsmoked
- ☐ Poppy seeds
- ☐ Star anise
- ☐ Tamarind paste
- ☐ Thai fry paste
- ☐ Turmeric powder

Oils
- ☐ Hazelnut oil
- ☐ Olive oil
- ☐ Sesame oil
- ☐ Walnut oil

Storecupboard essentials

- [ ] Apricots, dried
- [ ] Artichokes in olive oil, bottled
- [ ] Black olives
- [ ] Bouillon powder
- [ ] Chocolate, plain 70% solids
- [ ] Coconut, creamed
- [ ] Currants
- [ ] French dressing
- [ ] Horseradish sauce
- [ ] Lime leaves
- [ ] Miso paste
- [ ] Mushrooms, dried
- [ ] Mushroom ketchup
- [ ] Mustard, Dijon
- [ ] Mustard, wholegrain
- [ ] Peppers in olive oil, bottled
- [ ] Prunes
- [ ] Vinegar, balsamic
- [ ] Vinegar, red wine
- [ ] Vinegar, rice
- [ ] Vinegar, white wine
- [ ] Raisins
- [ ] Rice wine
- [ ] Sardines, canned
- [ ] Soy sauce, light
- [ ] Sundried tomatoes in olive oil, bottled
- [ ] Sweetcorn, canned
- [ ] Tabasco sauce
- [ ] Thai fish sauce
- [ ] Tomato passata
- [ ] Tomato paste
- [ ] Tomatoes, canned
- [ ] White wine, dry

Fruit

- [ ] Apples (eating and cooking)
- [ ] Apple juice, dry
- [ ] Blackberries
- [ ] Blueberries
- [ ] Carrot juice
- [ ] Grapefruit
- [ ] Lemons
- [ ] Limes
- [ ] Mangos
- [ ] Oranges
- [ ] Passion fruit
- [ ] Pears
- [ ] Raspberries
- [ ] Strawberries

Vegetables

- [ ] Asparagus
- [ ] Aubergines
- [ ] Avocados
- [ ] Beansprouts
- [ ] Beetroot
- [ ] Broad beans
- [ ] Broccoli
- [ ] Cabbage, green, red, spring
- [ ] Carrots
- [ ] Cauliflower
- [ ] Celeriac
- [ ] Celery
- [ ] Cherry tomatoes
- [ ] Courgettes
- [ ] Cucumbers
- [ ] Fennel, Florence
- [ ] Garlic
- [ ] Green beans
- [ ] Leeks
- [ ] Lettuce, romaine or cos
- [ ] Mangetout
- [ ] Mixed salad leaves
- [ ] Mushrooms, white and brown
- [ ] Onions, yellow and red
- [ ] Peas, frozen
- [ ] Peppers, green, red and yellow
- [ ] Shallots
- [ ] Spinach
- [ ] Spring onions
- [ ] Sprouted seeds
- [ ] Squash, acorn, butternut
- [ ] and gem
- [ ] Sweet potatoes
- [ ] Tomatoes
- [ ] Watercress

Dairy

- [ ] Feta cheese
- [ ] Fromage frais, fat-reduced
- [ ] Goats' cheese
- [ ] Haloumi light
- [ ] Hens' eggs
- [ ] Quails' eggs
- [ ] Tofu, marinated, silken and smoked
- [ ] Yoghurt, live natural low-fat

Meat

- [ ] Beef, lean and minced
- [ ] Chicken, bird, breasts and thighs
- [ ] Duck, breasts and smoked
- [ ] Ham, smoked and sliced
- [ ] Liver, calves' and chicken
- [ ] Pheasant, bird or breasts
- [ ] Pigeon, breasts
- [ ] Pork
- [ ] Rabbit
- [ ] Turkey
- [ ] Veal
- [ ] Venison, smoked and sliced

Fish

- [ ] Haddock, smoked
- [ ] Herring roes
- [ ] Prawns, cooked
- [ ] Salmon, fresh fillets
- [ ] Seafood
- [ ] Squid
- [ ] Trout
- [ ] Tuna, fresh fillets
- [ ] White fish fillets (haddock, cod, etc.)

Index

About the author

Ian Marber
MBANT Dip ION
Nutrition consultant, author, broadcaster and health journalist

Ian studied at London's Institute for Optimum Nutrition, and now heads The Food Doctor clinic at Notting Hill, London. He contributes to many of Britain's leading magazines and newspapers and has a regular column in *The Daily Telegraph*. Ian appears on the BBC, Channel 4, ITN News and GMTV, and on many radio shows. He has also made a 15-part series for the Discovery channel.

Undiagnosed food sensitivities in his twenties led to Ian becoming interested in nutrition. His condition was later identified as coeliac disease, a life-long intolerance to gluten. He is now an acknowledged expert on nutrition and digestion, and many of his clients are referred to his clinic by doctors and gastroenterologists.

Ian advises on all aspects of nutrition, and in particular on the impact that correct food choices can have. He is known by his clients to give highly motivational, positive and practical advice that can make a real difference to their well-being.

Ian's first book, *The Food Doctor – Healing Foods for Mind and Body*, co-written with Vicki Edgson, has sold one million copies and has been translated into nine languages. Ian subsequently wrote *The Food Doctor in the City*, and *In Bed with The Food Doctor*. In 2003 his book, *The Food Doctor Diet*, became an instant bestseller. Ian's plan was tested on Channel 4's *Richard and Judy* by three volunteers, who each lost a dress size in only three weeks. The feature was so popular that Richard and Judy tested Ian's subsequent book, *The Food Doctor Everyday Diet*, on six new volunteers over ten weeks, who all achieved similar results. Ian's plan has been hailed as a truly sensible, healthy approach to weight loss that really works.

Acknowledgements

To all at Dorling Kindersley, especially Mary-Clare Jerram and Penny Warren; to my editor, Susannah Steel, for her enthusiasm, support and the puppy; to my colleagues at The Food Doctor for their dedication, loyalty and hard work; special thanks to Michael da Costa and to Erika Andersson, my lovely assistant; to my friends for their love.

The publisher would like to thank Lucy Heaver for editorial assistance, Hilary Bird for the index and Francis Loney for the author photograph.

The Food Doctor Everyday Diet plan

Ian Marber's Everyday Diet weight loss plan is designed to help those people unable to visit Ian for a personal consultation to rebalance their body systems and lose weight healthily and for the long-term. The answer lies in identifying your metabolic rate, learning how to choose the right foods and, by doing so, rebalancing your metabolism to increase energy levels, motivation and ultimately weight loss. Yo-yo dieting disrupts metabolic rate, meaning that the next time you restrict what you eat you tend not to lose the pounds you have regained. This is why The Everyday Diet is just that, a diet plan that becomes a way of life as you follow 10 simple principles.

For more information, visit **www.theeverydaydiet.co.uk**

The Food Doctor food range

To help people make healthier food choices, our team of expert nutritional therapists are constantly adding to our exciting range of foods, which are available from many leading retailers, independent grocers and health food shops, or on-line (*see below*). The products are designed to help balance metabolism by providing a low Glycaemic Impact (GI) and restricting the release of blood sugar.

The range includes: Seed mixes, Dry Roasted Soya Nuts, Food bars, Muesli mix, Cereal mix, Porridge mix, High Bran and Seed Bagels, Omega-3 Yoghurt, Aloe Vera Yoghurt with pre-biotic, Essential Omega Seed Butter, Essential Omega Seed Oil, Mixed Cereal Puffed Crackers.

Visit our on-line shop at **www.thefooddoctor.com/shop**